Parent's Guide to

11+

Success

in all
11+ tests

Val Mitchell, Sally Moon

Contents

About the 11+ tests

The 11+ tests are used by schools to select the highest quality candidates from children who have applied to them directly.

Some schools will ask your child to take tests in English, maths, non-verbal and verbal reasoning, others will ask them to take just a few of these subject areas. There are several standardised tests that schools can use, although some local education authorities, examination boards and schools write their own. This book concentrates on the question styles, formats and levels of difficulty in the standardised tests, as well as providing some examples from other types of paper.

In many schools the final allocation of places is made after individual interviews have taken place. Advice about interview techniques and practice can be found on pages 66–69.

Subjects set in the 11+ tests

English

The English paper will consist of a reading test and may also contain a separate writing task. There is no standardised form of writing task and schools often create their own. The papers are generally divided in the following ways.

Reading

- Comprehension
- Grammar
- Punctuation
- Spelling

Writing

Maths

The Maths paper will consist of a written test and probably also a mental maths test, in which questions are read out. Calculators are not allowed for either test. Schools often write their own mental maths tests. The papers generally test the following skills.

Main test

- Numbers and their properties
- Calculations (including algebra)
- Fractions, decimals and percentages
- Working with charts and data
- Shape and space
- Measuring
- Data handling

Mental maths test

Non-verbal reasoning

Non-verbal reasoning tests involve solving puzzles and problems with visual or sequential patterns and their connections.

Verbal reasoning

Verbal reasoning tests involve solving puzzles and problems with letters, words or numbers and their connections.

Essential research

- Find out as much information as possible about your selected schools well in advance.
- Check the Ofsted inspection reports of your chosen schools online.
- Read the prospectus and check the website for each school.
- Arrange to visit the schools during a working school day.
- Before your visit, prepare a list of questions to ask.
- Note: Closing dates for applications vary, and some require a deposit against the first term's fees.

The Parent's Guide to 11+ Success **is designed to help you and your child prepare for the 11+ papers in five simple steps, so that your child can take the tests with confidence.**

The colour-coded sections in this guide divide up the process, making it easy to follow.

1 Test — What your child already knows

Set the Practice test in the centre of the book, then mark your child's answers together. This will show what they already know and where they need to do more work.

2 Track — Planning your child's practice

Fill in the grids to target the specific skills your child needs to develop and then plan their work. Reviewing these subject areas in Chapter *3 Reviewing your child's skills* will help you to do this and give you a good idea of the time they need to practise their skills before taking the test.

3 Review — Reviewing your child's skills

Work through the pages about the skills your child found challenging in the tests. Chapter *2 Planning your child's practice* will direct you to additional materials to support them in practising these skills.

4 Test — Testing for success

Work together through the example questions at the end of Chapter 3 to test their skills (these should be used in conjunction with the other support materials suggested).

Once you are both confident in your child's progress, look at the list of papers available on page 62 for final review and practice work before the tests.

5 Present — What your child has achieved

Work together to develop your child's presentation skills using the preparation, interview and discussion techniques on pages 64–69. If your child is asked to attend an interview at the school, good preparation gives them a chance to shine.

The tests and activities in this book are designed to help you guide your child towards success in their 11+ tests.

By taking the pull-out tests before your child begins their practice, and working through the activities, you will be able to prioritise the essential skills they will need to develop before taking their 11+.

The final chapter in the book will help to build your child's confidence as the test day approaches and to prepare them for the interview they may be asked to attend.

Understanding your child's strengths

As the tests in this book are designed to highlight your child's strengths, you will probably find that they do better in some subjects than others. It is typical for a child to be good at verbal reasoning if they have strong English skills and good at non-verbal reasoning if they have strong maths skills. The result of a non-verbal reasoning test is often a good indicator of the future potential of children who have English as an additional language.

Working with your child's results

The test grids in Chapter *2 Planning your child's practice* show which skills have been assessed for each subject. These grids link directly to the sections that cover the four different subject areas in Chapter *3 Reviewing your child's skills* to help you assess their current position.

When you have marked your child's test you will be able to see which skills are most important to review and Chapter 2 provides information about further practice materials to go to once you have done this.

Reviewing the skills

Chapter *3 Reviewing your child's skills* gives an overview of the skills needed in each subject. It also provides guidance on the style of questions your child may come across in the 11+ tests.

- *Subject area overviews* provide information on the skills coverage required and help clarify the standards expected.
- *Example questions* help you and your child to review their abilities in some of the more challenging skills.
- *Question types* demonstrate the variety of formats that may be used in the 11+ tests. These include…
  - multiple-choice answers
  - brief, standard written format
  - extended answers
  - oral delivery.

Practising the skills

Once your child has reviewed their skills and followed up with further practice where you feel this is needed, they are then ready to move on to working with timed 11+ practice tests. Chapter *4 Testing for success* details the process for working with these and guides you to suitable resources.

Preparing for the tests

When your child has completed their practice, Chapter *5 What your child has achieved*, on pages 64–69 can help you to support them in the final stages of their preparation. It contains…

- a 'countdown' of things to do and prepare
- interview advice on how to dress, relax and communicate
- some research techniques to support their interviews, discussions and writing tasks.

SATs practice

The SATs taken at the end of Year 6 also contain assessments in reading, writing and maths. The skills and questions outlined in this book will be useful to your child as they prepare for these assessments because they are derived from the same curriculum skills they are studying in school.

Taking tests can be stressful for your child and detailed planning can help to minimise this.

Although the timings below may seem a long time ahead of the 11+ tests, they suggest a realistic time-frame to make the preparations manageable.

One year before

- Confirm which schools you are applying for, and check on application closing dates (see page 4).
- Talk to your child's class teacher about their educational strengths and weaknesses. These include…
  - their predicted SATs Levels
  - their reading and spelling ages.

A year to nine months before

- Begin to prepare for the tests by…
  - assessing areas of strength and targeting areas of weakness using the pull-out tests in this book
  - planning your child's practice to fit in with family routines.
- Decide whether you want to employ a tutor to support your child in their learning or work together to create a programme (the materials suggested in this book will enable you to do this).
- Ensure that the planned work is weighted towards the skills your child will need to practise the most.
- Talk about incentives and rewards to make this practice a positive experience.
- Begin to prepare for interviews by planning suitable days out (see page 66).

One and two months before

- Try a practice interview (see pages 68–69).
- Build in some activities to reinforce skills (see pages 64–65).
- Rehearse basic maths and spelling at speed, to promote fast recall of information.
- Go over key skills in the areas highlighted by the pull-out tests.

One week before

- Give your child a rest from testing.
- Plan an educational visit that could act as a talking point at interview.
- Plan a route and timings for the day of the tests.
- Check information sent by the school, listing equipment you will need to provide (equipment will need to be taken in a see-through pencil case).
- Draw up a checklist for the day – an analogue watch is helpful for your child to see how much time they have left in a test.

One night before

- Prepare equipment and clothes.
- Encourage your child to do something relaxing.
- Make sure they have an early night.

The morning of the tests

- Go through your checklist.
- Make sure your child eats breakfast.
- Leave in good time.
- Encourage your child to enjoy the challenge and show off what they have learnt.

Taking the practice tests

Now that your child is ready to take the practice tests, it is important to make sure they have the right conditions to produce an accurate result.

These Practice tests (located in the 20-page pull-out booklet) will help you to identify the areas where your child will need further practice.

Timing

It is better for your child to do the tests in two mornings at a weekend when they are alert, rather than after a long day at school.

Allow the following times for each test, plus at least half an hour to get everything organised.

Day 1

Reading test: 40 minutes
Maths test: 30 minutes
BREAK
Non-verbal reasoning test: 30 minutes
Verbal reasoning test: 40 minutes

Day 2

Writing task: 45 minutes
BREAK
Mental maths test: about 15 minutes
Dictation test: about 15 minutes
Spelling test: about 15 minutes

Surroundings

Provide a quiet area without any distractions. Your child will need a clear table or desk to set out their materials.

Equipment

Make sure your child has the following items assembled before they begin…

- pen
- pencil
- eraser
- pencil sharpener
- ruler
- timer (this can be the timer on an oven or an alarm clock)
- analogue watch/clock (this will help your child to see how much time they have left)
- paper (for jotting ideas; start and finish times; Writing, Dictation and Spelling tests)
- tracing paper and a small mirror for the Maths and Non-verbal reasoning tests.

Giving the written tests

Structured tests

The Reading, Maths, Non-verbal reasoning and Verbal reasoning tests are located on pages 1–17 of the pull-out booklet.

All of these tests provide space for your child to write their answers. However, you should also provide spare paper for them to jot down ideas and workings.

Tracing paper and a small mirror are needed in the Maths and Non-verbal reasoning tests for trying translations, rotations and symmetry.

Note: You should mark these tests before giving the Mental maths test on the following day. This is because you will need to cut out pages 17–18 so that your child can fill in the Mental maths answer sheet as you read out the questions.

Writing task

The Writing task list is on page 17 of the pull-out booklet at the end of the Verbal reasoning test.

Review the list with your child and ask them to choose which task they want to write about. Give them several sheets of paper to complete the task as they will need spare paper to plan their work.

Giving the oral tests

You will need to be present after their break on Day 2 to read out the Mental maths, Dictation and Spelling tests.

Offer encouragement but don't be tempted to help by giving hints, because the tests are to find out what they can or can't do. If the results are not realistic they may not be adequately prepared for the 11+ tests.

Mental maths test

The Mental maths test is located on page 19 of the pull-out booklet. Your child should not look at this sheet before you give the test.

Give your child the Mental maths answer sheet from page 18 (cut out from the pull-out test booklet) before you begin.

Read out the questions clearly and slowly, giving your child time to write down their answer before moving on to the next question. You can repeat each question once. It is important that you do not share the test sheet with your child as this will not be allowed in the actual 11+ test.

Dictation and Spelling tests

The Dictation and Spelling tests are on page 20 of the pull-out booklet. Your child should not look at these tests before you read them out.

Give your child two plain sheets of A4 paper and a pencil to complete their tests. Read out the dictation passage and spelling words as instructed on the sheet.

Question types

If your child is taking a 'standardised' 11+ test, this will be provided in a multiple-choice or standard format. Both formats use multiple-choice questions, although they are answered in slightly different ways. On the multiple-choice version, a separate answer grid is used and on the standard version the answers are written on the test paper.

If the test is set by the school, local authority or an independent exam board they may be given a written format paper where they have to write their answers down.

The Practice papers in this book provide questions in both multiple-choice and written format to increase familiarity with both formats. Before your child begins the pull-out tests, discuss the question formats:

- **Multiple-choice questions** should be completed in *exactly* the way instructed in the question. Tell your child to read these questions very carefully, checking the number of choices required.

- **Written format questions** sometimes require one-word answers; other types require a phrase; and a third type will require a longer response with reference to the text. Point out the different question types so that your child is aware of them before they begin.

TIPS FOR SUCCESS

Read these tips to your child before they take the pull-out tests to focus their attention on what they are expected to do.

- Read each question twice.
- Check carefully what you are being asked to look for.
- Check carefully how you are instructed to give your answer: multiple-choice questions may ask you to write, circle or underline the answer.

Once your child has completed the Practice tests in the pull-out booklet, mark them together, following these instructions.

Structured tests

- Go to the *Answers* on pages 74–76 and mark the completed Practice tests by filling in the blank boxes in the 'Mark*' column. There is one mark allowed for each complete question – **there are no half marks**.

- Now turn to the *Reading, Maths, Verbal reasoning* and *Non-verbal reasoning grids* on pages 16–18.

- Transfer the marks to the 'Mark*' column.

- Add up the total for each subject section.

- Work out the percentages for each subject total, as directed in the Summary boxes on page 13.

Writing task

- Go to the *Writing grid* on page 20 if it is a fiction text, or on page 21 if it is a non-fiction text. Photocopy the grid so that you and your child can use it again later.

- Work through the grid one section at a time. You can do this together with your child.

- Read the text for each Level and then decide which most closely describes your child's piece of writing. For example, after you have read the Grammar section, you may feel that your child's text *contains a mixture of simple and complex sentences, imaginative vocabulary or vocabulary related to the text*. If this is the case, then you have decided that your child is working at Level 5.

  Note: Words highlighted in bold are explained in the Glossary on page 16.

- Once you have decided the Level that applies, ask your child to colour the relevant block in the Level column orange.

- Transfer your Levels for each section to the Summary boxes on page 13.

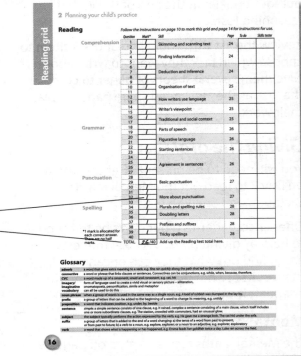

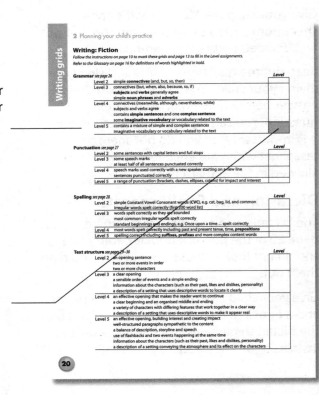

Mental maths test

- Go to the *Mental maths test answers* on page 76 and mark your child's completed *Mental maths answer sheet* by filling in the blank boxes in the 'Mark*' column. There is one mark allowed for each complete question – **there are no half marks**.

- Now turn to the *Mental maths grid* on page 17.

- Transfer the marks to the 'Mark*' column.

- Add up the total.

- Work out the percentage as directed in the Summary box on page 13.

Dictation test

- Go to the *Dictation grid* on page 19 and compare it with your child's completed *Dictation test*. Put a line through the box for each word spelt or punctuation mark included **correctly** (there must be capital letters in the correct places too).

- Add up the number of **blank** boxes (these are the words and punctuation marks that have been omitted or are **incorrect**).

- Subtract this total from 100. For example, if there are 7 errors (blanks), subtract this number from 100 to give a final score of 93.

- Transfer this final number to the Summary box on page 13. This is the percentage mark.

Spelling test

- Go to the *Spelling grid* on page 19 and compare it with your child's completed *Spelling test*. Tick each word spelt **correctly**.

- Add up the number of ticks to give the total on the line.

- Double the final total to give your child's percentage score and transfer this to the Summary box on page 13.

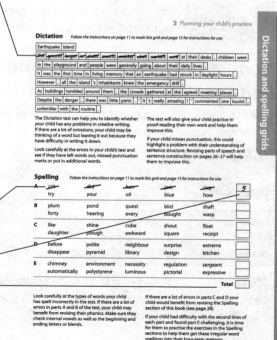

Summarising the tests

Now that you have assembled all the results from the pull-out tests, you can begin to plan your child's practice programme.

Understanding the Summary boxes

The Summary boxes will help you to build up a picture of the key areas your child will need to concentrate on in their 11+ practice. You should also view their results in relation to the information you found out from your research on page 7, 'Planning ahead'.

Reading, Maths, Verbal reasoning, Mental maths and Dictation tests

Refer to the list below to get an overview of your child's abilities in *reading, maths, verbal reasoning, mental maths* and *dictation*.

Up to 50%	Your child may need 9–12 months practice before attempting the 11+.
51–60%	Your child should feel encouraged that they will benefit from this book, although you will need to plan a practice programme carefully to target their weaker skills.
61–80%	Your child is already confident in many skills that will help them through the 11+ tests and will benefit from the support and guidance in this book.
81–100%	Your child is well on the way to success and the extra tips and support in this book will help them to get ahead of the rest!

Non-verbal reasoning, Writing and Spelling tests

Refer to the following chart to gain an overview of your child's abilities in *non-verbal reasoning, writing* and *spelling*.

Mostly Level 2 or up to 40%	Your child may need 9–12 months practice before attempting the 11+.
Mostly Level 3 or 40–50%	Your child should feel encouraged that they will benefit from this book, although you will need to plan a practice programme carefully to target their weaker skills.
Mostly Level 4 or 50–70%	Your child is already confident in many skills that will help them through the 11+ tests and will benefit from the support and guidance in this book.
Mostly Level 5 or 70–100%	Your child is well on the way to success and the extra tips and support in this book will help them to get ahead of the rest!

Summary boxes

Reading test

	Total	Percentage

Work out the percentage using this sum

$$\frac{Total}{40} \times 100 =$$

Maths test

	Total	Percentage

Work out the percentage using this sum

$$\frac{Total}{30} \times 100 =$$

Non-verbal reasoning test

	Total	Percentage

Work out the percentage using this sum

$$\frac{Total}{27} \times 100 =$$

Verbal reasoning test

	Total	Percentage

Work out the percentage using this sum

$$\frac{Total}{24} \times 100 =$$

Writing task

	Section	Level
Grammar		
Punctuation		
Spelling		
Text structure		

Mental maths test

	Total	Percentage

Work out the percentage using this sum

$$\frac{Total}{25} \times 100 =$$

Dictation test

	Total	Percentage

Spelling test

	Total	Percentage

After you have filled in the Summary boxes you will be able to get an overview of the subject areas where your child may need additional practice.

These are the areas where it will be helpful for them to use additional 11+ support material. Some useful resources are listed in this section.

Grids for the pull-out tests

The grids you have just completed are an essential tool in planning your child's 11+ practice.

Turn to the grids for the four structured tests (Reading, Maths, Non-verbal reasoning and Verbal reasoning) on pages 16–18 and look at the 'To do' column. You will see that questions are grouped into blocks.

- Colour the blocks in **green** where your child has answered **all** the questions **right.**
- Colour the blocks in **red** where they have answered **some or all** of the questions **wrong.**

Skill	Page	To do	Skills tester
Skimming and scanning text	24		
Finding information	24		
Deduction and inference	24		
Organisation of text	25		
How writers use language	25		

Example of Reading grid, marked with colour blocks

Red sections

Reviewing the skills

Together with your child, look at the sections on the grid (e.g. Comprehension, Grammar, Numbers and their properties, Letter level, Making connections) where you have coloured blocks in red. These are areas where they are likely to need more practice.

Now turn to Chapter *3 Reviewing your child's skills* (the page numbers are written next to the headings) to read through these sections. For example, if you have coloured 'Skimming and scanning text' in red, turn to the Comprehension section on page 24 and read through 'Skimming and scanning text'.

Talk through the skill together to see whether you feel your child has understood what was being asked.

It may just be that they misunderstood the question, although this type of mistake can highlight unfamiliarity with the skill and so they may still need additional practice.

Colour in the box next to this heading on the Reading grid to show you have looked at it together before you move on.

Planning their practice

We recommend that your child practises all the skills that have been highlighted by the test to build their confidence in answering these question types. Now that you are familiar with what these entail, you will find it easier to choose suitable practice materials. Page 62 lists a range of Letts books that cover all these skills by subject area and also provide additional tests and questions.

When to use the Skills tester and Question types questions

Go back to Chapter 3 after your child has been through their practice to check they are now confident about all the skills you highlighted on their grids. The Skills tester and Question types questions are provided to help you with this process.

The Skills tester questions tackle the more challenging areas of the subjects and are helpful to build confidence in specific skills. The Question types questions at the end of each section provide different question styles to help your child become familiar with the different formats the questions take. These are particularly useful if the school they are applying to sets their own tests.

Check your child's answers together, using the answers on pages 72–73, and colour the 'Skills tester' box on the grid green if they have answered correctly or red if they have answered incorrectly. This will help you to direct them to any skills that need some further practice in their final preparations.

Green sections

If your child has coloured the blocks in green, they should be well on the way to mastering these skills, so you may not want to go through the related sections as thoroughly. However, skimming quickly through the pages and trying out some activities will provide them with useful additional practice to speed up their test technique. Colour in the answer boxes on the grid, as you did for the 'red' questions, to keep a record of their progress.

Writing grids

The Writing grids will provide a helpful tool in the next step of your child's writing practice.

These grids are designed to give you a broad idea of your child's current abilities. To get the best picture of their progress in writing it is helpful to compare the Levels achieved here against information about their current Levels you have been able to obtain from the school to see if your findings match up.

Look at each section in the completed Writing grid (Grammar, Punctuation, Spelling and Text structure) and review the Levels against the list below.

- **Level 2:** You should review the English pages in the book (24–31) together, even if your child has answered some of the questions correctly in the Reading test, and plan a programme of writing practice.
- **Level 3:** We recommend that you review the English pages in the book (24–31) together. If your child feels confident with the skill, just suggest that they answer the Skills tester questions to reinforce their knowledge.
- **Level 4:** We recommend that your child answers the Skills tester questions to reinforce their knowledge.
- **Level 5:** Your child may wish to answer some of the Skills tester questions to build confidence in their skills.

If your child is at a Level 4 or below, we also recommend that they use further resources to develop their writing skills.

Mental maths summary

The results of the Mental maths test show your child's ability to manipulate numbers and number facts in their head (or with limited jottings). If they perform better in the mental test in contrast to the written test, this may indicate a difficulty with reading written instructions.

Look carefully at the Mental maths grid on page 17 to see which skills your child may need to practise. These could link to the skills you have highlighted in the pull-out test. Compare the two grids and make a note on the pull-out test grid of any sections where you feel your child may need additional practice.

Dictation summary

The Dictation test can help identify problems in your child's creative writing.

Look carefully at the errors in the test and see if they have left words out, missed punctuation marks or added additional words. The test is also a useful exercise for your child to practise proof-reading their own work.

If they have missed out punctuation marks, this could highlight a problem with their understanding of sentence structure. Revising sentence construction and parts of speech will help to improve this.

Spelling summary

Look carefully at the types of word your child has spelt incorrectly in the test. If you find a lot of errors in parts A and B of the test, they may benefit from revising their phonics skills.

If you find a lot of errors in parts C and D, your child could benefit from revising the common spelling rules.

If they had difficulty with the second lines of each section and found part E challenging, they are likely to need to increase their familiarity with irregular word spellings.

Essential practice support

These titles have been created to support your child in the key subject areas needed for the 11+.

- Letts 11+ English Success
  9781844195459
- Letts 11+ Maths Success
  9781844195466
- Letts 11+ Non-Verbal Reasoning Success
  9781844195480
- Letts 11+ Verbal Reasoning Success
  9781844195473

Understanding the summaries and grids

Reading grid

Reading

Follow the instructions on page 10 to mark this grid and page 14 for instructions for use.

	Question	Mark*	Skill	Page	To do	Skills tester
Comprehension	1		Skimming and scanning text	24		
	2					
	3		Finding information	24		
	4					
	5					
	6		Deduction and inference	24		
	7					
	8					
	9		Organisation of text	25		
	10					
	11					
	12		How writers use language	25		
	13					
	14		Writer's viewpoint	25		
	15					
	16		Traditional and social context	25		
	17					
Grammar	18		Parts of speech	26		
	19					
	20		Figurative language	26		
	21					
	22		Starting sentences	26		
	23					
	24		Agreement in sentences	26		
	25					
	26					
	27					
Punctuation	28		Basic punctuation	27		
	29					
	30					
	31		More about punctuation	27		
	32					
	33					
Spelling	34		Plurals and spelling rules	28		
	35		Doubling letters	28		
	36					
	37		Prefixes and suffixes	28		
	38					
	39		Tricky spellings	28		
	40					
	TOTAL	/40	Add up the Reading test total here.			

*1 mark is allocated for each correct answer. There are no half marks.

Glossary

adverb	a word that gives extra meaning to a verb, e.g. She ran *quickly* along the path that led to the woods.
connective	a word or phrase that links clauses or sentences. Connectives can be conjunctions, e.g. while, when, because, therefore.
CVC	a word made up of a *consonant*, *vowel* and *consonant*, e.g. cat, hit
imagery/ imaginative vocabulary	form of language used to create a vivid visual or sensory picture – alliteration, onomatopoeia, personification, simile and metaphor can all be used to do this
noun phrase	when a group of words is used in the same way as a single noun, e.g. *A load of rubbish* was dumped in the lay-by.
prefix	a group of letters that can be added to the beginning of a word to change its meaning, e.g. untidy
preposition	a word that indicates position, e.g. under, by, beside
sentence	*simple:* a simple sentence consists of one clause, e.g. It rained. *complex:* a sentence consisting of a main clause, which itself includes one or more subordinate clauses, e.g. The station, crowded with commuters, had an unusual glow.
subject	the subject typically performs the action expressed by the verb, e.g. He gave me a strange look. The cat hid under the sofa.
suffix	a group of letters that is added to the end of a word changing: a) the tense of a word from past to present, or from past to future; b) a verb to a noun, e.g. explore, explorer; or a noun to an adjective, e.g. explorer, exploratory
verb	a word that shows what is happening or has happened, e.g. Emma feeds her goldfish twice a day. Luke ran across the field.

Maths

Follow the instructions on page 10 to mark this grid and page 14 for instructions for use.

Numbers and their properties

Calculations

Fractions, decimals and percentages

Working with charts and data

Shape and space

Measuring

*1 mark is allocated for each correct answer. There are no half marks.

Question	Mark*	Skill	Page	To do	Skills tester
1		Ordering and rounding whole numbers	32		
2					
3		Number patterns and sequences	32		
4		Factors and multiples	32		
5		Adding and subtracting whole numbers	33		
6		Multiplying and dividing whole numbers	33		
7					
8		Solving problems involving the four operations	33		
9					
10		Algebra	33		
11		Fractions	34		
12		Fraction calculations	34		
13		Decimals	34		
14		Finding equivalents	34		
15		Percentage calculations	34		
16		Ratio and proportion	34		
17		Charts and graphs	35		
18					
19		Finding the mode, median, mean and range	35		
20		Probability	35		
21		2-D and 3-D shapes	36		
22					
23		Angles	36		
24		Perimeter, area and volume	36		
25		Coordinates	36		
26		Reflection, translation and rotation	37		
27		Patterns and puzzles	37		
28		Length, capacity and weight	38		
29					
30		Time	38		
Total	/30	Add up the Maths test total here.			

Mental maths

Follow the instructions on page 11 to mark this grid and page 15 for instructions for use.

Numbers and their properties

Calculations

Fractions, decimals and percentages

Working with charts and data

Shape and space

Measuring

*1 mark is allocated for each correct answer. There are no half marks.

Question	Mark*	Skill	Page	To do
1		Ordering and rounding whole numbers	32	
2		Number patterns and sequences	32	
3		Factors and multiples	32	
4		Adding and subtracting whole numbers	33	
5				
6		Multiplying and dividing whole numbers	33	
7				
8		Solving problems involving the four operations	33	
9		Algebra	33	
10		Fractions	34	
11		Fraction calculations	34	
12		Decimals	34	
13		Finding equivalents	34	
14		Percentage calculations	34	
15		Ratio and proportion	34	
16		Finding the mode, median, mean and range	35	
17		Probability	35	
18		2-D and 3-D shapes	36	
19		Angles	36	
20		Perimeter, area and volume	36	
21				
22		Patterns and puzzles	37	
23		Length, capacity and weight	38	
24				
25		Time	38	
Total	/25	Add up the Mental maths test total here.		

Non-verbal and verbal reasoning grids

Non-verbal reasoning

Follow the instructions on page 10 to fill in this grid and page 14 for instructions for use.

	Question	Mark*	Skill	Page	To do	Skills tester
Making connections	1		Common connections	40		
	2		Connections of direction, angle and symmetry	40		
	3		Finding similarities and differences	41		
	4					
	5		Spotting distractions	41		
Breaking codes	6					
	7		Codes with two letters	42		
	8					
	9					
	10		Codes with three letters	43		
	11					
Finding relationships	12		Changing shapes	44		
	13		Number and proportion	44		
	14		Moving and connecting shapes	44		
	15		Reflecting shapes	45		
	16					
	17		Rotating shapes	45		
Spotting patterns	18		2 × 2 grids	46		
	19					
	20		3 × 3 grids	47		
	21					
Completing sequences	22		Repeating patterns	48		
	23					
	24		One-step patterns	48		
	25					
	26		Two-step patterns	49		
	27		Number patterns	49		
	TOTAL	/27	Add up the Non-verbal reasoning test total here.			

*1 mark is allocated for each correct answer. There are no half marks.

Note: Non-verbal reasoning questions often require a number of different skills to solve them. Refer to the Non-verbal reasoning connections grid on page 61 to find out about skills that are commonly linked.

Verbal reasoning

Follow the instructions on page 10 to fill in this grid and page 14 for instructions for use.

	Question	Mark*	Skill	Page	To do	Skills tester
Letter level	1		Making words across a gap	52		
	2		Making two new words	52		
	3		Analogies with letter changes	52		
	4		Complete the third pair	52		
	5		Reordering letters into words	52		
Word level	6		Closest in meaning	53		
	7		Different in meaning	53		
	8		Analogies by word meaning	53		
	9		Incomplete words	53		
	10		Odd one out	53		
	11		Compound words	54		
	12		Word pairings	54		
	13		Double meanings	54		
	14		Word creation	54		
Letter and number patterns	15		Letters with number codes	55		
	16		Words with number codes	55		
	17		Alphabet pair sequences	55		
	18		Letter codes	55		
	19		Number sequences	55		
	20		Number patterns and equations	56		
	21					
	22		3 × 3 grids	56		
Logic	23		True statement	56		
	24		Deduction	56		
	TOTAL	/24	Add up the Verbal reasoning test total here.			

*1 mark is allocated for each correct answer. There are no half marks.

Dictation

Follow the instructions on page 11 to mark this grid and page 15 for instructions for use.

| Earthquake | Island |

| The | ground | began | to | shake | around | midday | when | workers | were | at | their | desks | , | children | were |

| in | the | playground | and | people | were | generally | going | about | their | daily | lives | . |

| It | was | the | first | time | in | living | memory | that | an | earthquake | had | struck | in | daylight | hours | . |

| However | , | all | the | island | 's | inhabitants | knew | the | emergency | drill | . |

| As | buildings | tumbled | around | them | , | the | crowds | gathered | at | the | agreed | meeting | places | . |

| Despite | the | danger | , | there | was | little | panic | . | ' | It | 's | really | amazing | ! | ' | commented | one | tourist | , |

| unfamiliar | with | the | routine | . |

The Dictation test can help you to identify whether your child has any problems in creative writing. If there are a lot of omissions, your child may be thinking of a word but leaving it out because they have difficulty in writing it down.

Look carefully at the errors in your child's test and see if they have left words out, missed punctuation marks or put in additional words.

The test will also give your child practice in proof-reading their own work and help them improve this.

If your child misses punctuation, this could highlight a problem with their understanding of sentence structure. Revising parts of speech and sentence construction on pages 26–27 will help them to improve this.

Spelling

Follow the instructions on page 11 to mark this grid and page 15 for instructions for use.

A	cot	did	hen	jam	cup	
	try	your	oil	blue	how	
B	plum	pond	quest	blot	shaft	
	forty	hearing	every	bought	wasp	
C	like	shine	cube	shout	float	
	daughter	plough	awkward	square	receipt	
D	before	polite	neighbour	surprise	extreme	
	disappear	pyramid	library	design	kitchen	
E	chimney	environment	necessity	regulation	sergeant	
	automatically	polystyrene	luminous	pictorial	expressive	
					Total	

Look carefully at the types of words your child has spelt incorrectly in the test. If there are a lot of errors in parts A and B of the test, your child may benefit from revising their phonics. Make sure they check internal vowels as well as the beginning and ending letters or blends.

If there are a lot of errors in parts C and D your child would benefit from revising the Spelling section of this book (see page 28).

If your child had difficulty with the second lines of each part and found part E challenging, it is time for them to practise the exercises in the Spelling sections to help them get these irregular word spellings into their long-term memory.

Writing: Fiction

Follow the instructions on page 10 to mark these grids and page 13 to fill in the Level assignments.

Refer to the Glossary on page 16 for definitions of words highlighted in bold.

Grammar *see page 26*

		Level
Level 2	simple **connectives** (and, but, so, then)	
Level 3	connectives (but, when, also, because, so, if)	
	subjects and **verbs** generally agree	
	simple **noun phrases** and **adverbs**	
Level 4	connectives (meanwhile, although, nevertheless, while)	
	subjects and verbs agree	
	contains **simple sentences** and one **complex sentence**	
	some **imaginative vocabulary** or vocabulary related to the text	
Level 5	contains a mixture of simple and complex sentences	
	imaginative vocabulary or vocabulary related to the text	

Punctuation *see page 27*

		Level
Level 2	some sentences with capital letters and full stops	
Level 3	some speech marks	
	at least half of all sentences punctuated correctly	
Level 4	speech marks used correctly with a new speaker starting on a new line	
	sentences punctuated correctly	
Level 5	a range of punctuation (brackets, dashes, ellipses, colons) for impact and interest	

Spelling *see page 28*

		Level
Level 2	simple Constant Vowel Consonant words (**CVC**), e.g. cat, bag, lid, and common irregular words spelt correctly (first 200 word list)	
Level 3	words spelt correctly as they are sounded	
	most common irregular words spelt correctly	
	standard beginnings and endings, e.g. Once upon a time… spelt correctly	
Level 4	most words spelt correctly including past and present tense, time, **prepositions**	
Level 5	spelling correct including **suffixes, prefixes** and more complex content words	

Text structure *see pages 29–30*

		Level
Level 2	an opening sentence	
	two or more events in order	
	two or more characters	
Level 3	a clear opening	
	a sensible order of events and a simple ending	
	information about the characters (such as their past, likes and dislikes, personality)	
	a description of a setting that uses descriptive words to locate it clearly	
Level 4	an effective opening that makes the reader want to continue	
	a clear beginning and an organised middle and ending	
	a variety of characters with differing features that work together in a clear way	
	a description of a setting that uses descriptive words to make it appear real	
Level 5	an effective opening, building interest and creating impact	
	well-structured paragraphs sympathetic to the content	
	a balance of description, storyline and speech	
	use of flashbacks and two events happening at the same time	
	information about the characters (such as their past, likes and dislikes, personality)	
	a description of a setting conveying the atmosphere and its effect on the characters	

Writing: Non-fiction

Follow the instructions on page 10 to mark these grids and page 13 to fill in the Level assignments.

Refer to the Glossary on page 16 for definitions of words highlighted in bold.

Grammar *see page 26*

		Level
Level 2	simple **connectives** (and, but, so, then)	
Level 3	connectives (but, when, also, because, so, if)	
	subjects and **verbs** generally agree	
	simple **noun phrases** and **adverbs**	
Level 4	connectives (whereas, furthermore, in addition)	
	subjects and **verbs** agree	
	contains **simple sentences** and one **complex sentence**	
	some technical vocabulary or vocabulary related to the subject	
Level 5	contains a mixture of simple and complex sentences	
	technical vocabulary or vocabulary related to the subject	

Punctuation *see page 27*

		Level
Level 2	some sentences with capital letters and full stops	
Level 3	some speech marks	
	at least half of all sentences punctuated correctly	
Level 4	speech marks used correctly with a new speaker starting on a new line	
	sentences punctuated correctly	
Level 5	a range of punctuation (brackets, dashes, ellipses, colons) for impact and interest	

Spelling *see page 28*

		Level
Level 2	simple Constant Vowel Consonant words (**CVC**), e.g. cat, bag, lid, and common irregular words spelt correctly (first 200 word list)	
Level 3	words spelt correctly as they are sounded	
	most common irregular words spelt correctly	
Level 4	standard vocabulary linked to non-fiction structure, e.g. advert for 'sale', 'reduction'	
	most words spelt correctly including past and present tense, time, **prepositions**	
Level 5	spelling correct including **suffixes**, **prefixes** and technical words	

Text structure *see pages 29–30*

		Level
Level 2	a heading and/or introduction, basic address elements in letters	
	some information set out in the correct order	
	a section that relates to a heading	
Level 3	mostly correct structure for the non-fiction type	
	similar pieces of information grouped together in sections	
	sections all link to their headings	
Level 4	correct structure for the non-fiction type	
	text grouped together in paragraphs and headings (appropriate to text type) in a logical order	
	a breakdown of heading levels (appropriate to text type)	
Level 5	purpose and context of the text clear	
	text grouped in a thoughtful way supported by relevant argument and detail	
	headings laid out clearly and imaginatively (appropriate to text type)	
	style or writing adapted to the text type: personal or formal	

11+ tests are based on the Primary Curriculum and Learning Objectives for English and Maths to Year 6 and this section provides a summary of the skills that your child will be expected to have.

Verbal reasoning and non-verbal reasoning do not have a prescribed curriculum, although some of the skills are derived from those taught in English and Maths.

Together with your child, review the sections highlighted by their Practice tests from the pull-out booklet to decide which skills they should practise to build their confidence. The questions on the Question types pages and at the end of each section can be used for this practice to check coverage in key areas.

The subject areas

English

The English pages in this section review the skills most frequently assessed in the 11+ tests.

Although comprehension is tested in the SATs Reading paper at the end of Year 6, the 11+ tests also ask specific questions on grammar, punctuation and spelling.

The standardised 11+ Reading tests break the subject up into these separate categories (although they are not identified by headings, the instruction text makes the section breaks clear) so you will easily be able to review the pages in this section against both the pull-out test and any practice papers you obtain.

In addition to the Reading tests, your child is likely to be set a Writing task. They will need to be familiar with the different writing genres to enable them to tackle the task. These genres are explained on pages 29–30. They will also need to be confident in structuring texts in these different styles, as detailed in the guidelines on page 23.

Maths

The Maths pages in this section review the skills most frequently assessed in the 11+ tests.

In addition to the main Maths test, your child will probably be given a Mental maths test in which the questions are read out. Calculators are not allowed for either test.

The 11+ Maths tests are based on the Primary curriculum tested in the SATs. They include a number of problem-solving questions to test children's ability to combine skills from different areas of maths.

Non-verbal reasoning

There is no prescribed curriculum for non-verbal reasoning. Non-verbal reasoning tests are set to assess children's ability to think around problems, make connections and work logically.

The Non-verbal reasoning pages in this section break the subject into a number of categories that can be linked to the questions in standardised Non-verbal reasoning tests.

Because of the nature of these problems, inevitably a number of skills are needed to solve them. The chart on page 61 shows how non-verbal reasoning skills interconnect. This is a helpful tool when your child is having difficulty solving particular questions, as often they may be missing a skill that is common to several questions. For example, a number of problems involve understanding rotations and reflections.

Verbal reasoning

Because there is no curriculum for verbal reasoning, the pages in this section look at the most frequently occurring examples set in the 11+ tests.

In addition to testing for an ability to solve problems logically, the questions assume a competent level of spelling and vocabulary, and the ability to apply basic maths principles in calculations and algebra to solve problems. The spelling and maths principles are both covered in the English and Maths sections of this chapter.

Planning

Whatever test your child is tackling, they should always leave time at the beginning of the test to plan their work and time at the end to check it. Work that is presented in an organised way using clear English generally gains better marks.

Planning and checking work is important in all the tests but especially important in English writing tasks. Share the following guidelines with your child to help them with the writing tasks in this book and in preparation for the 11+ tests (see page 17 of the pull-out test).

Writing tasks

Genre

Think about the subject you have been given and jot down the key writing styles and structures needed for this genre.

Non-fiction texts

Beginning Introduce what you are going to talk about.

Middle Explain your ideas, opinions, or the facts you are interested in.

End Sum up what you have written about.

Stories and plays

Beginning Introduce the characters in your story, and the place where it is set.

Middle Explain what happens, what the characters do, and how they solve their problems.

End Explain how the story ends and what happens to the characters.

Paragraphs

If you are writing continuous text, make sure your work is split into paragraphs…

- the first paragraph should set the scene
- each paragraph should have a clear main idea
- each paragraph should follow on logically from the last
- the final paragraph should summarise and conclude the piece of writing.

Rules of five

To ensure a range of different sentence structures, check that your work includes sentences that start with…

1 a noun or pronoun
2 an adjective
3 a verb
4 an adverb
5 a preposition.

To ensure a range of different punctuation structures, check that your work includes…

1 full stops at the ends of sentences
2 capital letters for sentence starts and proper nouns
3 commas
4 a question mark or exclamation mark
5 another appropriate punctuation mark such as speech marks, ellipses, a semi-colon, a colon, brackets.

Editing

Read through your work to check that it makes sense. Then ask yourself the following questions…

- Have I included everything I wanted to say?
- Have I told the readers everything they need to know?
- Have I used some interesting vocabulary?
- Is my work easy to read?

Check the text to…

- make sure no words are missing
- check your spellings and easily confused words.

Comprehension

'Comprehension' questions always relate to a passage provided with the test. Questions in this section of the test look for the ability to read for meaning. There is a range of question types under the heading of 'comprehension' that assess differing skills.

Skimming and scanning text

Skimming gives the reader a quick overview of the text and scanning is used to find particular words or information. The skill needed is the ability to pick out the *key words* to gain a general sense of what is happening, rather than to look for detail. This can be developed with repeated practice.

Features that should be reviewed when skimming are…

- title, to find out about the subject
- nouns, to find out about the subject content
- verbs and adjectives, to convey moods
- first and last lines of paragraphs, to understand what each section of text is about.

Features that should be reviewed when scanning are…

- words relating to the subject of the question, e.g. if the question asks for information about Vikings being seafarers, words should be looked for that link to the sea: ocean, fjord, boat, sail, etc.
- separate areas of the text, such as lists and glossaries.

Finding information

Texts come in a wide variety of formats. Understanding how these different structures work is a key skill in being able to retrieve information quickly and accurately.

Elements that should be reviewed in non-fiction texts are…

- what type of text (genre) it is
- the key features of that text type, e.g. if the question asks what ingredients would be needed to make a cake, the ingredients list should be referred to
- technical vocabulary or words related to the subject, e.g. if a question asks about electrical safety, words such as 'danger' and 'conductor' would be useful.

Elements that should be reviewed in non-fiction texts are…

- who the characters are
- what is happening
- where it takes place
- why certain events happen or why people act in a certain way
- adjectives and adverbs, to pick up clues about moods and feelings.

Deduction and inference

Deduction questions expect the reader to reach a conclusion based on clear information. Inference questions look for an ability to respond to a text and reach a conclusion.

Deduction questions should be tackled by looking for words in the text that point to the answer…

- When asked about where a piece is set, words should be looked for that relate to the climate, terrain or the objects people use.

- When asked to speculate about what might happen next, words relating to the sequence of events, such as 'before' or 'then' could be useful.

Inference questions should be tackled by looking for clues in the text that help to work out what is going on by…

- identifying distractions put in to trip the reader up
- carefully checking details before reaching a conclusion.

Organisation of text

Understanding how sentences and paragraphs are linked is a key skill in developing more advanced skills in interpretation. The way a text is organised can provide clues to its meaning and purpose.

The organisation of fiction texts should be analysed by…

- considering how the text opens
- identifying the sequence of events
- checking for flashbacks, or where two events are happening at the same time, e.g. where Snow White is at the cottage when the witch and the dwarves are racing back to save her
- noting how the text finishes.

The organisation of non-fiction texts should be analysed by…

- considering the layout within the text style
- identifying headings and sub-headings
- checking for diagrams and other ways the information has been divided and highlighted
- noting conclusions and summaries.

How writers use language

Questions about how writers use language test the ability to comment on how the writer's choice of words affects the meaning of a text.

A writer's use of language can by understood by considering…

- the title, and how this affects expectations of the text to follow
- nouns, adjectives, verbs and adverbs, which set the mood and themes
- the voice, to consider how the writer is thinking

- emotive words, where the writer is purposefully leading the reader in a certain direction.

Writer's viewpoint

Answering questions about a writer's viewpoint demonstrates an ability to distinguish between fact and opinion.

A writer's use of language can by understood by…

- looking for key phrases such as, 'I think', or 'In my opinion' or text within speech marks
- considering the balance between fact and opinion
- reviewing the supporting evidence
- identifying any language that shows strong emotion
- looking for rhetorical questions and inclusive language, e.g. 'We should find a way forward together!'

Traditional and social context

Questions on traditional and social contexts test the ability to work out when and where a text was written.

Information relating to when and where a text was created can by found by looking for clues about…

- *time*: in relation to what people wear, what they do and what they use
- *place*: in relation to distinctive place names, climate, terrain, dialect, point of view.

Looking for ideas in texts that are different to your child's own experience are a useful way of finding clues to the answer in these question types.

Grammar

Grammar is the name for all the rules relating to how words interact with each other. Questions in the grammar section of the test look for the ability to identify different word types, language techniques and features, as well as agreement of verbs and tense.

Parts of speech

'Parts of speech' are the different types of words that can be found in a sentence. Questions in this area assess understanding of the function of these words.

Terms that should be identified are…

- nouns and adjectives
- verbs and adverbs
- prepositions
- connectives and conjunctions
- pronouns and articles.

Starting sentences

These questions test understanding of the variety of ways in which sentences can begin and how different word types relate to each other.

Changing the start of a sentence can alter its tone…

- Prepositions can be used for a reassuring start, e.g. Once upon a time…
- Verbs and adverbs can make the beginning lively, e.g. Wildly leaping into the river…
- Nouns and adjectives introduce the subject quickly, e.g. Hungry lions often eat…
- Speech can be used to draw the reader in, e.g. 'Watch out!' cried the teacher.

Agreement in sentences

A vital aspect of understanding how sentences are constructed is consistency in agreement and tense.

Key points of sentence agreement include…

- Singular nouns need singular verbs.
- Tense needs to be consistent within a passage of text.

Figurative language

Questions on identifying and commenting on figurative language test the ability to assess how effectively descriptions are written.

Key features to look for are…

- similes and metaphors
- personification
- onomatopoeia
- alliteration and assonance
- rhyme.

It is important to be familiar with a variety of technical language terms: your child's school should be able to provide a list of terms they are expected to know in each year group.

Reading and writing poetry is a good way to build skills in working with figurative language. Reading, because poetry contains examples of a variety of these techniques, and writing because creating poetry to practise using figurative language helps to consolidate learning.

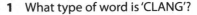 SKILLS TESTER

1 What type of word is 'CLANG'?

   A onomatopoeia　　　**B** homophone　　　**C** simile

   D alliteration　　　**E** personification

2 Choose the best word to complete this sentence and circle the letter underneath.

   Yesterday, I　dig　dug　digging　digged　will dig　the garden.

   　　　　　　A　**B**　　**C**　　　**D**　　　**E**

Punctuation is the name for all the marks used in sentences that allow them to be read clearly and unambiguously. Questions in the punctuation section of the test look for the ability to identify different ways to begin and end sentences, as well as the various ways to divide them and make them easier to read.

Basic punctuation

Questions about basic punctuation test understanding of how to organise and divide clauses and sentences…

- capital letters and full stops, e.g. It rained.
- capitalisation for proper nouns and 'I', e.g. 'When it rained on Tuesday, Fred and I got wet in Bradford.'
- question marks and exclamation marks, e.g. 'Will it rain today? I'm covered in snow!'
- commas for lists, e.g. Don't forget your wellingtons, raincoat, hat and gloves.
- commas to separate clauses, phrases and adjectives, e.g. The clouds, which were a thunderous black, cast a shadow over the houses.

More about punctuation

An understanding of the various ways sentences are constructed is important when reviewing and structuring text. More advanced punctuation questions test this understanding.

Knowledge of the function of the following punctuation marks is assumed…

- speech marks, including the rule to follow for 'new speaker, new line', e.g. 'Put your bikes in the shed, or they'll get wet!' shouted Dad.
  'Give me a chance,' yelled Manjil. 'I've only just got back.'
- apostrophes for possession and omission, e.g. Gill's rucksack was behind the neighbours' compost bin. Her brother knew she'd never find it there.
- semi-colons and colons, e.g. Balvir gave her Dad a rugby ball for his birthday; rugby was his favourite sport. Dad's collection was amazing: he had two bags of golf clubs, three squash rackets, two hockey sticks and a set of goal posts.
- dashes, hyphens and ellipses, e.g. The umbrella – pink with yellow spots – was missing. Nobody had spotted the four-letter word. Jane wondered where it would all end…
- parentheses (brackets), e.g. Shemar: It's awfully dark outside. (appearing stage right).

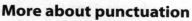

SKILLS TESTER

1 Copy the sentence below, correcting any punctuation errors.

mr barry helped rob to pick up the tin its lid the pieces of paper and the named glove lying next to them

2 Pick out the section with no punctuation errors. If all the sections are correct, choose X.

James wanted the	roller, skates.	he desperately wanted	to be in the Team.	
A	B	C	D	X

Spelling can be broken into stages of learning, from simple phonics to words with common patterns, followed by more rules and irregular spellings. Questions in the spelling section of the test look for knowledge of these rules and exceptions to identify and correct errors.

Plurals and spelling rules

The rules on plural spellings apply to nouns and also to the related verbs.

Familiarity with the following rules is expected…

- For most nouns, 's' is added, e.g. computers.
- If a word ends in a consonant and a 'y' (e.g. lady), the 'y' is changed to an 'i' and 'es' is added (i.e. ladies). If a word ends in a vowel and a 'y' (e.g. turkey), only 's' is added (i.e. turkeys).

- If a word ends in 'ess', 'ch', 'th', 'sh' or 'x', 'es' is added to make the plural, e.g. boxes. Some words ending in 'o' take 'es', e.g. tomatoes.
- For many words that end in an 'f', the 'f' changes to 'v' and 'es' is added (e.g. wolf changes to 'wolves'). Sometimes only an 's' is added (e.g. chef becomes chefs).
- Some words stay the same (e.g. sheep), and some change completely (e.g. mouse changes to mice). These exceptions should be learnt…

Doubling letters

Doubling letters follows a clear set of rules, knowledge of which is often tested.

Knowledge of the following rules is assumed…

- If a word has a short vowel sound (e.g. shop), the final letter is doubled in order to keep the sound short (shopping). However, if a word has a long vowel sound (e.g. hope), the 'e' is dropped and 'ing' is added with no double letter (hoping).
- If a word ends in 'er' or 'ur', and the main stress is on the last syllable (e.g. occur), the 'r' is doubled when the ending 'ing' or 'ed' is added to retain the stress (occurring).

Prefixes and suffixes

Knowledge of prefixes and suffixes is important to spelling but also relates to grammar. Prefixes and suffixes include…

- prefixes that give words an *opposite* meaning including 'un', 'dis' and 'anti'
- common prefixes such as 'trans', 'tele'; some of these define number, e.g. 'bi'
- suffixes where 'ly' is added changing an *adjective* to an *adverb*, e.g. 'quick' changes to 'quickly'

- suffixes where 'er' and 'est' are added to show *comparison*, e.g. quick, quicker, quickest
- common suffixes, such as 'tion', 'less', 'ful'.

Tricky spellings

It is possible to learn some rules about difficult spellings but familiarity only comes through reading a wide variety of texts.

There are some spelling types that occur frequently…

- Homophones – words that sound the same but have different meanings, e.g. weather, whether.
- When a 'g' or 'c' is followed by an 'e', 'i' or 'y', it has a soft sound. This is important for words such as 'giant' as it distinguishes between using a 'j' or a 'g'.
- Letter groups such as 'ght', 'tion/sion', 'tch', 'tious/cious' are very common, but they are not sounded in the way they are written, e.g. bought, tension.
- Words with silent letters, e.g. 'knob' and 'autumn'.
- The letter groups 'ur', 'ir', and 'er' often have the same sound, e.g. fur, fir, further.

SKILLS-TESTER

Pick the words that are correctly spelt to fill the gaps.

The garden … watched the fish … in the muddy pond.

A nome, swimming   **B** gnome, swiming   **C** nome, swiming

D gnome, swimming   **E** knome, swimming

The Writing task is generally a separate test in the 11+. This task can be set on a fiction or non-fiction topic. It tests the ability to structure and style a text in a way that is appropriate to the genre.

Fiction

Writing stories

A number of basic elements are looked for in story writing. Work that shows an ability to combine these skills in an imaginative and integrated way would gain higher marks.

Structure: A story has…
- a beginning, middle and end
- a logical development of the story; more complex stories could involve flashbacks or two events happening at once
- descriptions of the characters and setting
- at least two characters
- dialogue
- a resolution.

Style: The story must…
- have characters that are believable
- use a range of figurative language for effective description
- use adjectives, adverbs and a variety of sentence structures to make the story come to life.

Writing plays

Plays can be created in any of the genres used in story writing. It is very important to use stage directions in order to achieve a high mark.

Structure: A play has…
- a plot
- a cast list of characters
- scenes (rather than chapters)
- only dialogue and action telling the plot
- stage directions to control the action.

Style: A play can use…
- dialect and accents
- characterisation through speech such as catch phrases.

Writing poems

It is unlikely that poetry will be set as a writing task, although knowledge of the different types is important as different schools can introduce new questions to test children's overall abilities.

Structure: Types of poetry structure include…
- free verse: monologues, conversation poems, list poems
- visual poems: calligrams and shape poems, concrete poems
- structured poems: haiku, cinquains, rapping, limericks.

Style: A poem can use…
- word patterns such as rhyme, rhythm, repetition, alliteration, assonance, onomatopoeia
- imagery such as simile, metaphor
- imaginative and unusual combinations of word and form.

Non-fiction

Writing discussion texts

The important element in any discussion text is a reasoned argument.

Structure: A discussion text has…
- a statement of the issues involved
- arguments *for*, with supporting evidence
- arguments *against*, with supporting evidence
- a summary with a concluding viewpoint.

Style: A discussion text using…
- the present tense
- noun-phrases such as, 'some people believe …'
- nouns that categorise a theme such as environment, habitat
- interesting connectives such as however, despite
- quotations.

Writing explanatory texts

The important element in any explanatory text is a logical progression through a process.

Structure: An explanatory text…
- has a statement to introduce the topic being explained
- shows progression in a series of steps that are organised in paragraphs
- is sometimes supported by diagrams.

Style: An explanation can be written…
- in the present tense
- using connectives such as first, next, following, that
- using conditionals such as because, so, consequently
- in an impersonal style.

Writing instructional and procedural texts

It is important that the instructions in instructional and procedural texts are easy to follow and have a defined outcome.

Structure: Instructional and procedural texts…
- begin with a short paragraph outlining the purpose of the instructions
- give numbered, simple instructions
- contain bullets for non-sequential elements
- include diagrams if they are relevant and necessary to support the text.

Style: An instructional or procedural text can be written…
- in the present tense
- using imperative verbs such as mix, blend, construct
- using precise vocabulary
- including additional advice such as 'Decorate with chocolate curls for a special occasion.'

Writing non-chronological reports

The important elements in writing non-chronological reports are the clear organisation and categorisation of information.

Structure: A non-chronological report has…
- an opening paragraph that introduces the whole topic
- paragraphs grouped under different headings, e.g. for a report about looking after a cat, tips on feeding would all come under one heading
- a clear opening sentence for each paragraph to outline its contents
- connectives to link ideas between paragraphs.

Style: A report can be written…
- in the present tense
- usually in the third person, i.e. he, she, it, they
- with the passive voice, e.g. The cat is a relative of the lion.
- using comparison and facts to create precise descriptions rather than effect.

Persuasive writing

The important factor in persuasive writing is to create a convincing argument.

Structure: Persuasive writing…
- can begin with a statement of the position being promoted
- has the information organised in a way that supports a particular view
- ends with a persuasive conclusion.

Style: Persuasive writing can be written…
- in the present tense
- with rhetorical questions, e.g. 'Could you live without one?'
- with repetition to enforce points
- with connectives, to make it look as if one point proves another, e.g. 'This shows that…'
- with emotive language to manipulate the reader, e.g. 'This is an outrageous situation'.

Recount texts

The important factor in recount texts is to be informative *and* entertaining.

Structure: A recount text has…
- an introduction that sets the scene
- events told in the order in which they happen
- time connectives that link the events such as after that, next
- a closing comment to sum up the text.

Style: Recount texts are written…
- usually in the past tense
- in the first or third person, i.e. I, we or he, she, it, they.

Letter writing

The important factor in writing letters is to communicate the subject of the letter clearly.

Structure: Letters include…
- the address
- the date
- a salutation (or greeting)
- paragraphs to convey the content
- a subject (informal letters)
- an ending, dependent on the salutation, e.g. when the letter begins 'Dear Sir,' it should end 'Yours faithfully'.

Style: Letters should use…
- precise language for formal letters
- an informal style of speech for informal letters.

The 11+ Reading tests are often all set as multiple-choice questions in a variety of formats. Familiarity with this is helpful to build speed and confidence.

When your child is going through practice papers it is important that they review the instruction text, usually at the top of a series of questions, before circling, underlining or filling in the answer.

Comprehension

The question examples below relate to the text on pages 26–30.

Use the information on the previous pages to answer these questions. Circle the correct answer.

Single choice

Most questions only ask for one option to be chosen from a selection of four or five possible answers, as in the example below.
Alternatively, the question may ask for the answer to be written out.

1   Which of these features is likely to be found in a story?

   A cast list   **B** imperative verbs
   C flashback   **D** salutation   **E** diagrams

Double choice

Some questions ask for more than one option to be chosen from a selection of four or five possible answers, as in the example below.

Alternatively, the question may ask for the answers to be written out.

2   Which two types of text use diagrams?

   1 explanatory texts   **A** 1 and 3 only
   2 plays   **B** 1 and 5 only
   3 recounts   **C** 4 and 5 only
   4 stories   **D** 2 and 3 only
   5 instructional and   **E** 3 and 5 only
        procedural texts

Grammar

Most questions only ask for one option to be chosen from a selection of four or five possible answers, as in the example below. Alternatively, the questions may ask for the answer to be written out in full.

3   What part of speech is the word 'fiction' in the following sentence.

   Fantasy and science fiction are some of the genres than may occur in story writing.

   A pronoun   **B** preposition   **C** adverb   **D** metaphor   **E** noun

Punctuation

Most questions are set out as sentences with the phrases broken up into sections to analyse, as in the example below. Alternatively, the question may ask for the answer to be written out in full.

4   Pick out the section in the sentence below in which the punctuation is incorrect.

   "Using three things in adverts is very effective" announced Tyler Muffin,

   | **A** | **B** | **C** |

   the Marketing Manager, as he gestured at the screen.

   | **D** | **E** |

Spelling

Most questions are set out as sentences with the phrases broken up into sections to analyse, as with punctuation questions. Occasionally the question may ask for the answer to be written out in full.

5   Rewrite this sentence, correcting the spelling and punctuation.

   the aliens were hoping abowt on the rooves when a reallie cool ship floo bye

Numbers and their properties

'Numbers and their properties' underpins all of mathematics.
Questions on this group of skills look for evidence of a clear understanding
of different types of numbers and how to use them in a range of situations.

Ordering and rounding whole numbers

To compare sizes of numbers, a sound knowledge of the decimal place value system is expected.
The ability to arrange numbers into an ascending or descending order as instructed is important.

Important skills in ordering are…

- 'crude' or 'rough' ordering, which involves looking for the number of digits and whether there are decimals (which would make it a small number)
- detailed ordering, which involves looking at place value and then ordering from the highest to the lowest, e.g. 10 001, 1200, 1001.

Important skills in rounding are…

- rounding to the nearest 10, e.g. numbers that would round to 520 would be: 515, 516, 517, 518, 519, 520, 521, 522, 523 and 524
- rounding to the nearest hundred or thousand
- rounding numbers that are halfway between, e.g. numbers ending in 5, 50 or 500 (which always round up to the 10, 100 or 1000 above).

Number patterns and sequences

Questions relating to number patterns and sequences require the identification of the mathematical rule that extends a sequence. They involve looking for repeating patterns.

Number and pattern skills that should be learnt are…

- looking at gaps between numbers in a sequence to find how the sequence continues. For example, 3 4 6 7 9 10 12 … …
  The 'gaps' between the numbers alternate here, i.e. there is a gap of '1' after the first, third and fifth numbers and a gap of '2' after the second, fourth and sixth, so the answer is 13 and 15. The 'gaps' may be multiples as well as additions.
- common sequences: even numbers; odd numbers; square numbers, e.g. 1, 4, 9, 16; cube numbers, e.g. 1, 8, 27, 64; triangular numbers, e.g. 1, 3, 6, 10; prime numbers, e.g. 2, 3, 5, 7, 11.

Factors and multiples

A good working knowledge of the multiplication tables is the key requirement when working with questions on factors and multiples.

The ability to apply these basic factor and multiple skills is assumed…

- common factors: numbers that divide into another number with no remainder
- common multiples, including numbers from 1 to 12 and their multiplication tables. This also includes multiplications that use a combination of these calculations, such as multiples of 20: 40, 60, 80 (using the $2 \times$ table and adding '0').

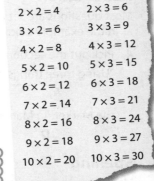

$2 \times 2 = 4$	$2 \times 3 = 6$
$3 \times 2 = 6$	$3 \times 3 = 9$
$4 \times 2 = 8$	$4 \times 3 = 12$
$5 \times 2 = 10$	$5 \times 3 = 15$
$6 \times 2 = 12$	$6 \times 3 = 18$
$7 \times 2 = 14$	$7 \times 3 = 21$
$8 \times 2 = 16$	$8 \times 3 = 24$
$9 \times 2 = 18$	$9 \times 3 = 27$
$10 \times 2 = 20$	$10 \times 3 = 30$

SKILLS TESTER

1 Place these numbers in ascending order, with the smallest to the left.

   3, -5, 7, 2, 0, -4, 1, -1

   [ ] [ ] [ ] [ ] [ ] [ ] [ ] [ ]

2 Identify which of these pairs of numbers are both factors of 16.
   A 32, 48   **B** 8, 2   **C** 2, 32   **D** 10, 6   **E** 4, 24

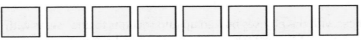

The topic of 'Calculations' is all about how numbers are processed to solve problems. Questions on this group of skills test the ability to select the correct mathematical operation, calculate an answer and perform the calculation accurately.

Adding and subtracting whole numbers

Quick retrieval of learnt information with accurate calculations are the skills that are looked for in these question types.

Important skills in adding and subtracting are...

- knowing and using number bonds to 10 and 100 as a starting-point for calculations
- using doubles and near-doubles, halves and near-halves, e.g. knowing that 8 + 8 = 16 helps when adding 9 + 8 and 7 + 8
- deciding in which order to perform simple calculations, e.g. adding a smaller number to a larger one
- understanding common terms that indicate the operation being used
- adding and subtracting using written methods
- checking and estimating answers by performing inverse calculations.

Multiplying and dividing whole numbers

Rapid recall of multiplication tables is essential for tackling both long and short multiplication and division.

Multiplying and dividing skills should include...

- multiplying and dividing by 10, 100 and 1000
- multiplying by 9, 99 and 999
- repeated doubling, such as 7 + 7, 14 + 14, 28 + 28
- using powers for repeated multiplication, e.g. 2^4 means $2 \times 2 \times 2 \times 2$
- short division, e.g. 3654 ÷ 7 worked in a written method
- column and grid multiplication
- short cuts for division, including when dividing by 5, double, then divide by 10, e.g. 775 ÷ 5 becomes 1550 ÷ 10 = 155
- checking and estimating answers by performing the inverse calculation.

Solving problems involving the four operations

A good working knowledge of how the operations of addition, subtraction, multiplication and division work is expected.

Confidence should be demonstrated in the following skills...

- completing multiplication and division operations before addition and subtraction in multi-part problems
- matching calculations of similar types, such as calculations with the same answer or written in the same form
- adding brackets to a calculation in the appropriate places.

Algebra

Answering algebra questions successfully demonstrates an ability to use letters or abstract shapes to represent numbers and solve problems.

Basic skills in algebra include...

- substitution, when a letter is substituted for a given value to help solve an equation
- using formulae, involving replacing letters with numbers in equations and looking at the pattern of results to identify the maths involved.

SKILLS TESTER

1   Look at this number fact.
    655 × 42 = 27 510
    What is 21 × 655?

    A 17 355   **B** 676   **C** 13 755
    D 697   **E** 52 371

2   8n − 16 = 80. What is the value of n?

    A 40   **B** 8   **C** 64
    D 12   **E** 104

'Fractions, decimals and percentages' are all different ways of showing the steps between whole numbers. Questions on this group of skills test the ability to understand comparisons and proportions.

Fractions

Familiarity with factors and multiples is an important element in being able to tackle questions on fractions quickly and accurately.

Important skills involving fractions are…

- understanding equivalent fractions and lowest terms. This involves working with facts such as: $\frac{1}{4} = \frac{2}{8} = \frac{4}{16}$. The lowest term here is $\frac{1}{4}$.
- ordering fractions by writing a given set of fractions as equivalents and ordering them in ascending or descending order.

Fraction calculations

Being familiar with the terms 'numerator' and 'denominator' and an ability to find common denominators are important when carrying out fraction calculations.

Useful skills when performing fraction calculations include…

- an ability to use 'tricks' or shortcuts, e.g. when working out $\frac{3}{4}$ of the amount, divide the total by 4 then take the answer away from the total
- working out a 'whole' number from one of its fractions
- finding what fraction one amount represents of another.

Decimals

Working with decimals requires an ability to work with fractions of a unit.

Confidence should be demonstrated in the following skills…

- adding and subtracting decimals; remembering to line up decimal points when using a column method
- multiplying and dividing decimals; working with the digits as whole numbers and then reinstating the decimal points
- rounding decimals to a given number of decimal places.

Finding equivalents

Questions involving equivalents anticipate knowledge of how to convert fractions, decimals and percentages from one form to another.

Skills in understanding equivalents include…

- rapid recall of the correspondence between the three standard forms
- working with fractions of percentages such as $13\frac{1}{2}\%$
- ordering a combination of fractions, decimals and percentages.

Percentage calculations

Working with percentages requires the understanding that one 'whole' is represented by 100%.

Basic skills in calculating percentages include…

- working out 1% of an amount, then multiplying by 100 to get 100%
- finding the percentage of an amount, such as the percentage of eggs that have been broken in a box
- calculating how much something has increased or decreased by percentage, e.g. a 50% reduction in a sale.

Ratio and proportion

Ratio and proportion skills look for the ability to compare different numbers in a variety of contexts.

Important aspects of ratio and proportion include…

- understanding the link between ratios and fractions
- proportional division: dividing a number to a given ratio.

SKILLS-TESTER

A three-litre bottle of washing-up liquid is mixed with water in the ratio of 1 : 11. How many two-litre bowls can be filled after it has been diluted?

A 18 **B** 36 **C** 11

D 12 **E** 1

The questions on this group of skills test the ability to analyse and interpret data presented in various forms.

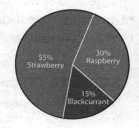

Charts and graphs

Quick retrieval of information from charts and graphs is the skill required in these question types.

Important skills are…

- reading and interpreting bar charts and pictograms
- reading and interpreting pie charts
- reading and interpreting time-based and conversion graphs
- comparing information extracted from bar charts and pictograms
- comparing information extracted from pie charts
- comparing information extracted from time-based and conversion graphs.

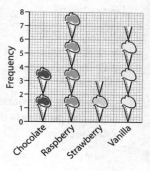

Finding the mode, median, mean and range

The skill being tested in mode, median, mean and range questions is the ability to differentiate between these terms, extract the information from tables, charts and graphs, and then calculate each using the appropriate operation.

Confidence should be demonstrated in the following skills…

- ordering the numbers to be worked with (including any repeated numbers)
- finding the mode of a set of given data using tally charts or ordering skills
- finding the median of a group of given data by ordering, and understanding that with an even set of numbers, the median falls between the two central values

- finding the mean of a set of given data by addition and division
- finding the range by subtracting the lowest value from the highest.

Probability

Understanding the principle of probability in terms of how likely something is to happen is the key to working with this skill.

Familiarity with the following processes is expected…

- calculating probabilities by following the principles used for fraction calculations
- adding up a range of probabilities and understanding that the total must equal one
- applying the principles of expected outcomes.

SKILLS TESTER

The table shows the number of eggs laid by Charlie's chickens over a two-week period.

Day	1	2	3	4	5	6	7	8	9	10	11	12	13	14
Eggs laid	1	10	6	5	3	4	5	5	4	9	8	5	0	2

1 What is the median number of eggs laid?

   A 10   **B** 4.5   **C** 5.5   **D** 9   **E** 5

2 What is the range in this egg data?

   A 10   **B** 4.5   **C** 5.5   **D** 9   **E** 5

3 If two in every eighteen customers in the newsagents receives a free lottery ticket, how many times will Rajesh have to visit the shop to expect to get three tickets?

Shape and space

'Shape and space' covers both 2-D and 3-D shapes and their properties. Questions on this group of skills are looking for an ability to think visually and to apply this to coordinates and transformations.

2-D and 3-D shapes

The skill being tested in questions on 2-D and 3-D shapes is the ability to apply a sound knowledge of shapes and their properties to solve problems.

An ability to apply these skills is expected…

- identifying the properties of common 2-D and 3-D shapes and retrieving this information at speed
- using the terms: parallel, symmetrical, adjacent, perpendicular to, with regard to 2-D shapes.

Angles

Questions set on angles are looking for an understanding of the vocabulary, size and measurement of angles with accuracy.

Confidence should be demonstrated in the following skills…

- using the properties of acute, obtuse and reflex angles and applying these to problem-solving
- finding unknown angles by using knowledge of angles on a straight line, at the centre of a circle and within a regular shape
- using prior knowledge of the properties of 2-D shapes such as opposite corners of parallelograms being equal
- estimating the approximate size of a given angle.

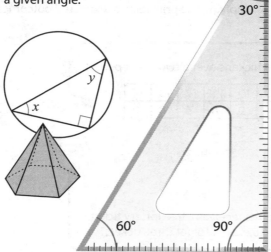

Perimeter, area and volume

Being able to demonstrate a working knowledge of perimeter and areas of 2-D shapes; the surface area and volume of 3-D shapes are the skills being assessed.

Familiarity with the following perimeter and area skills is expected…

- calculating the perimeters of regular 2-D, irregular 2-D and compound shapes
- joining and separating shapes to simplify calculations or find missing measurements
- using division to solve perimeter problems involving regular shapes where the perimeter and one side is given
- applying the correct formula to work out areas of simple shapes including triangles, squares and rectangles, e.g. $\frac{1}{2}$ base × height is the area of a triangle
- deciding which units are appropriate to the calculation such as answers relating to area being in cm^2, m^2.

Familiarity with the following volume skills is expected…

- applying the rule that multiplying length × breadth × height gives the volume of 3-D shapes
- calculating surface area by the addition of the area of each face of a 3-D shape.

Coordinates

Understanding how coordinates are used to locate points in four quadrants drawn on a grid is the key skill being tested in this question type.

The ability to apply these skills is required…

- following a defined series of steps to plot coordinates or define their positions
- using knowledge of decimals to estimate the position of points between gridlines
- identifying and plotting both parallel and perpendicular lines, then predicting further points that extend beyond these
- predicting where the final corner of a square will be when three corners are given on a grid.

Reflection, translation and rotation

Questions on reflection, translation and rotation all test the ability to move 2-D shapes in different ways. The original shape is called the object and the new shape after the transformation is called the image. Using a mirror and tracing paper is important when working in this area, and these may be supplied in the 11+ tests. It can be helpful to practise with these materials since they can make the transformations easier to visualise and remember.

The ability to demonstrate the following skills is expected…

- reflecting different 2-D shapes on a grid with a given mirror line
- identifying lines of symmetry and finding them in 2-D shapes
- moving a shape vertically and horizontally to new locations on a grid; both of these may be needed to move a shape diagonally
- rotating a 2-D shape through a given angle when the centre of rotation is clearly marked
- identifying what rotational order a shape has, i.e. in how many positions does the shape look the same when rotated? For a rectangle the answer would be '2'.

Patterns and puzzles

The key skill looked for in questions on patterns and puzzles is the ability to link different areas of mathematics and logical thinking.

The essential areas of learning are…

- breaking the problems into manageable steps
- combining skills from different areas of mathematics
- looking for repeated patterns and sequences
- predicting how many small shapes will fit into a larger shape.

SKILLS TESTER

1   This is half of an isosceles triangle. What are the coordinates of the third angle of this shape?

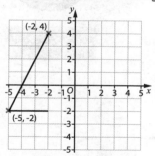

2   Look at the pattern below. If the sequence continues in the same way, how many red ellipses will be in pattern 5?

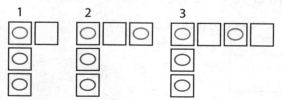

3   If the sequence in this pattern continues in the same way, how many squares will be in pattern 10?

'Measuring' looks at the standard units of measurement in daily use. Questions on this group of skills are testing the ability to measure length, capacity, weight and time and solve problems relating to these.

Length, capacity and weight

The key skills tested involve the ability to work with units of length, weight and capacity, to estimate, convert and adjust.

Confidence should be demonstrated in the following skills…

- converting units of measure from whole numbers to decimals, e.g. changing 30cm to 0.3m
- converting metric to imperial measures, e.g. changing grams to pounds
- reading scales such as those on measuring jugs, weighing scales, speedometers
- adjusting
- estimating the weight of common items, e.g. a banana weighs about 100g (and not 1kg).

Time

A clear understanding of the language of time and the passing of time are being tested in questions of this type.

The ability to apply these skills is expected…

- telling the time on 12-hour and 24-hour clocks
- calculating according to the fact that there are 60 seconds in a minute and 60 minutes in an hour
- converting time shown on an analogue clock to digital time, including the 24-hour clock
- calculating according to the fact that calendars function in relation to months and years
- calculating differences in time by counting back into the past or forward into the future
- multiplying and dividing time, e.g. the cooking time for a turkey is 180 minutes, so dividing by 60 will give the number of hours it will take.

SKILLS TESTER

1   Convert 2.75 litres of milk to millilitres. If this milk is poured into 50 millilitre cups, how many cups will be filled?

   A 1375   **B** 5.5   **C** 555   **D** 55   **E** 275

2   Write the time for twelve o'clock (midnight) on a 24-hour digital clock in the boxes below.

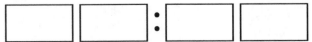

Comprehension

Read this text carefully before answering the questions below.

The Tin

How it all began

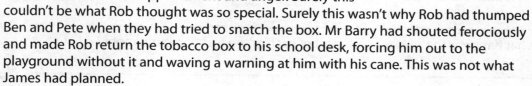

Peering inside the small tin box, James saw tiny pieces of paper, each with a Roman numeral written in spidery script. He felt a mixture of disappointment and anger. Surely this couldn't be what Rob thought was so special. Surely this wasn't why Rob had thumped Ben and Pete when they had tried to snatch the box. Mr Barry had shouted ferociously and made Rob return the tobacco box to his school desk, forcing him out to the playground without it and waving a warning at him with his cane. This was not what James had planned.

Shaking the silent box, James had felt certain that there would be money inside. Notes: he was convinced of it before he first distracted Robert by sending him off to the office to see his non-existent Mum. He had hoped for a brown ten-shilling note, at the least. Then he could buy the football boots that had shouted 'BUY US' from the shop window in the High Street. Without his own boots, he could never play for the school or county team and his dream of running out onto the pitch at Old Trafford one day would be in ruins.

By now Robert would be hot-footing it down the corridor. He would know it was all a wild goose chase. Would Robert come to the classroom? James tipped the box up, letting the small scraps spill all over the floor scattering like confetti. He walked out, slamming the door violently so that the paper pieces seemed to leap away across the floor.

There was a name for boys like James.

Write your answers on the lines provided. When you are given a choice of answers, write the letter for the answer you think is correct, i.e. A, B, C, D, E or X.
Do not write in the 'Mark' column.

Mark

1 How did James feel in the first paragraph?

_____

2 Why did James think that there would be notes, not coins, in the box?

A because the box rattled   **B** because he had opened the box before

C because the tin was too small for coins

D because the box was quiet when shaken

E because he saw tiny pieces of paper

3 What was written on the pieces of paper?

A little messages   **B** cartoons   **C** nothing – they were blank

D romantic letters   **E** numerals

4 Which of these words is closest in meaning to the word 'script'?

A cobweb   **B** torn   **C** writing   **D** tomb   **E** religion

Reading test

Mark

5 In the list below, find the names of two other boys in James' class who are mentioned in the story.

1 Rob   **2** James   **3** Barry   **4** Pete   **5** Notes

A 1 and 2   **B** 1 and 3   **C** 3 and 4   **D** 4 and 5   **E** 1 and 4   _____

6 Why do you think the boy tipped the box up onto the floor?

_____

7 How would Robert be returning to class?

A limping   **B** slowly   **C** rapidly   **D** gracefully   **E** peacefully   _____

8 What does the text tell us that James must have to get into the school football team?

_____

9 What happens to the box at the start of each of the first two paragraphs?

_____

10 Which genre do you think best fits this passage?

A horror   **B** fantasy   **C** fairy story   **D** legend   **E** adventure   _____

11 Do you think this extract is from the beginning, the middle or the end of a story? Give a reason for your answer.

_____

12 What do you think 'a wild goose chase' means?

A wandering around   **B** walking like a goose

C going to look for something that isn't there

D chasing after someone   **E** getting really angry   _____

13 Think of another word the writer could have used instead of 'ferociously'?   _____

14 What does the last line reveal about how the writer feels about the boy?

The writer…

A thinks the boy calls his friends names.

B thinks the boy is thoughtful.   **C** thinks the boy has a cool name.

D likes the boy.   **E** thinks the boy is a thief.   _____

15 Do you think that the writer likes Mr Barry, the teacher? Back up your view with evidence from the text.

_____

_____

16 What does the second to last line in paragraph 1 tell the reader about when this passage was set?

_____

_____

17 Which country do you think this passage is set in?

A Australia   **B** India   **C** Italy   **D** Britain

X None of the above   _____

2

Grammar

18 What part of speech is the word 'violently'?

   A verb   **B** noun   **C** pronoun   **D** adverb   **E** preposition

19 What part of speech is the word 'would' in
Would Robert come to the classroom?

   A question **B** verb   **C** noun   **D** preposition   **E** adverb

20 Which of these phrases demonstrates alliteration?

   A tried to snatch the box   **B** waving a warning at him

   C a brown ten-shilling note **D** scattering like confetti

   E it was all a wild goose chase

21 Which phrase shows an example of personification?

   A the football boots that had shouted 'BUY US'

   B letting the small scraps spill   **C** written in spidery script

   D hot-footing it down the corridor   **X** none of the above

Choose the correct word from the lists below to complete each sentence.

22 … eyes slowly filled with tears as he noticed his precious
numbers all over the classroom floor.

   A Mr Barry   **B** After   **C** His   **D** Gradually **E** Some

23 … he was as rich as the other boys in his class was a constant
pastime for James.

   A Wishing   **B** Sometimes **C** Quickly   **D** Money   **E** Now

24 No sooner … James shut the door, when Robert appeared
round the corner.

   A have   **B** did   **C** will   **D** had   **E** to

25 … go to the office if you like and get your letters as I am going
there anyway.

   A I'm   **B** When   **C** I'll   **D** I've   **E** He's

26 Football boots or new shoes … my options for my next
birthday present.

   A is   **B** are   **C** was   **D** and   **E** be

27 The boys … not available to explain their actions.

   A is   **B** were   **C** was   **D** and   **E** be

Reading test

Punctuation

Mark

28 Pick out the section or sections where punctuation is missing.
If all the sections are correct, choose X.

Rob had loved his grandad,   an Oxford Professor of Maths,
        A   **B**

who had taught him about trigonometry algebra
                 C

and differential calculus.
      D   **X**

Copy the sentences below, correcting any punctuation errors.

29 Mr barnes helped rob to pick up the tin the lid the pieces of paper and the
named glove lying next to them

_____

_____

30 why had someone been so mean rob the youngest in the class could not hold
back the tears

_____

_____

31 It was quiet before rob started to scream Why Why Why

_____

32 Select the pair of words between which the colon should be placed.

My schoolbag always contains the same items a pencil case my football kit
a packed lunch and fruit juice

A schoolbag: always   **B** contains: the   **C** same: items

D items: a   **E** case: my

33 Pick out the section where an apostrophe is missing. If all the sections are
correct, choose X.

James box was now closed,   its contents   having been returned
             A   **B**   **C**

and the lid securely shut.
       D   **X**

Spelling

34 Copy the sentence below, correcting any spelling errors.

The boys were playing with the batterys and the torchs under the archs in the
school chapel.

_____

_____

4

35 Copy the sentence below, correcting any spelling errors.

Mark

The begining of the leson was a disaster as Rob rumaged for the pieces of papper.

_____

_____

36 Which two words are incorrectly spelt in the sentence below?

The computer game was addictive; the asassin had to get to the treasury and avoid being seen before transfering the package.

A computer, asassin   **B** asassin, treasury   **C** transfering, computer
D addictive, transfering   **E** asassin, transfering

37 Pick out the prefixes and suffixes that complete this sentence.

He quick… …agreed with the …suitable secretary, while giving the small… of smiles.

A est	dis	en	er
B en	re	un	est
C ly	dis	an	ing
D ed	ex	en	er
E ly	dis	un	est

38 Copy the sentence below, adding the missing suffixes.

He was hopeful that the energy-save… light bulbs would final… stop the care… waste of electricity.

_____

_____

39 Copy the sentence below, correcting the spelling.

The musem's maintanance schedeul was very comprehensive, containing a list of extrordinary jobs, including cleaning the mummy.

_____

_____

40 Only one of the following sentences has no spelling errors. Can you find it?

A I am definately correct.
B The messenger had there military information.
C The exhibition contained a display, remembering the 1900 diaster.
D The caterpillar track left indentations in the dessert sand.
E Please don't postpone the meeting at the restaurant.

TEST ENDS

Maths test

Write your answers on the lines provided. When you are given a choice of answers, you will need to circle the letter (A, B, C, D or E) you think is correct. Some questions ask you to mark a diagram. Please use an extra sheet of paper for your workings. *Do not write answers in the 'Mark' column.*

You may not use a calculator.

Mark

Numbers and their properties

1 Round 475 to the nearest ten. _____

2 Look at this list of numbers.

   3099   3900   3110   3009   3190   3109

   Put the three smallest numbers in order of size, starting with the smallest.

   _____   _____   _____
   smallest   ➜   *largest*

3 What is the next number in the sequence?

   2   9   16   23… _____

4 What are the factors of 21? _____ _____ _____ _____

Calculations

5 Add together 257, 38 and 109. _____

6 What is the remainder when 48 is divided by 5? _____

7 Calculate 73×8 _____

8 Lucy and Fabio were playing darts. Together they scored 123. Fabio threw a 19, a double 18 and a double 6 with his first three darts. How many points did Lucy score? _____

9 On one winter's night the temperature in London was 2°C. The temperature in Aberdeen was 7°C lower than London. The temperature in Glasgow was 2°C higher than Aberdeen. What was the temperature in Glasgow? Circle the correct letter.

   A 9°C   **B** -3°C   **C** -7°C   **D** -5°C   **E** 11°C

10 Calculate the value of x in the equation $3x + 7 = 22$ $x =$ _____

Fractions, decimals and percentages

11 Which is the larger fraction, $\frac{7}{12}$ or $\frac{3}{5}$? _____

12 James prints out 20 photographs. $\frac{4}{5}$ are blurred so he throws them away. He puts the rest in an album. How many photographs does James put in the album? _____

13 $17.43 - 4.56 =$ _____

6

Mark

14 Write the decimal 0.8 as a fraction in its lowest terms.

15 Calculate 20% of 650.

16 The ratio of boys to girls in the school gym club is 3 : 5. There are 25 girls.
How many boys are there in the gym club?

Working with charts and data

Some parents were asked to choose their favourite sport. The results were displayed on the bar chart below.

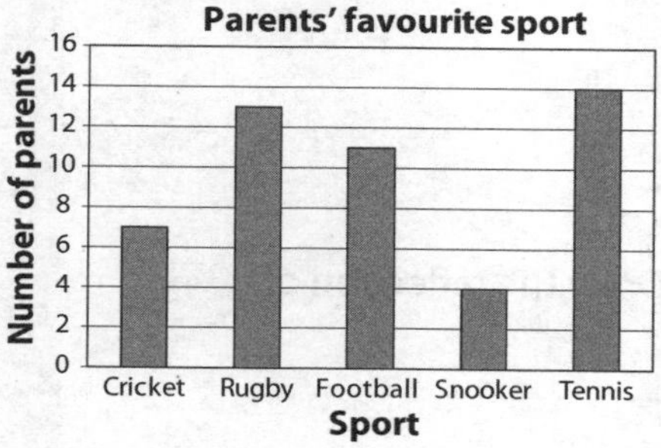

Parents' favourite sport

17 How many parents chose cricket?

18 How many parents took part in the survey altogether?

19 Look at this set of test scores.

16   12   11   14   19   15   16   13   18   16

What is the modal score? Circle the correct letter.

A 8   **B** 15   **C** 16   **D** 18   **E** 19

20 A fair eight-sided spinner numbered 1 to 8 is spun. What is the probability of the spinner landing on a multiple of 3? Circle the correct letter.

A $\frac{1}{2}$ **B** $\frac{1}{3}$ **C** $\frac{1}{4}$ **D** $\frac{3}{8}$ **E** 1

Shape and space

21 How many corners are there on a cube? Circle the correct letter.

A 6   **B** 8   **C** 10   **D** 12   **E** 14

22 Which of the shapes listed below has only 2 lines of reflective symmetry?
Circle the correct letter.

A Square   **B** Equilateral triangle   **C** Pentagon   **D** Cube   **E** Rectangle

23 How many degrees are there in half a turn? Circle the correct letter.

A 90°   **B** 180°   **C** 270°   **D** 280°   **E** 360°

Mark

24 Look at this shape. What is the perimeter of the shape?

5cm

2cm

3cm

8cm

_____ cm

25 What are the coordinates of the point X?

(_____ , _____)

26 Move the shape 2 squares down, 1 square to the left. Draw the reflection of the translated shape in the mirror line AB.

A

B

27 Draw the missing pattern in this series of shapes.

Measuring

28 Write 3.5 metres in centimetres.

_____ cm

29 Which of these containers holds about 5 millilitres of liquid?
Circle the correct letter.

A Bucket   **B** Mug   **C** Medicine spoon   **D** Saucepan   **E** Soup bowl

30 I set out from home at 08:50. My journey takes four-and-a-quarter hours.
At what time does my journey finish?
Give your answer in 12-hour clock time.

_____

TEST ENDS

Making connections

Look at the five images in each row. Work out what connects *four* of the images and makes the other image the odd one out. Circle the letter under the image most *unlike* the others.

Example

 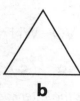

   a   b   c   d   (e)

*Shapes a, b, c and d are all regular shapes; shape e is an irregular shape.
The shape most unlike the others is* **e***.*

Now have a go at these similar questions. Circle the letter under the image that you think is most unlike the others.

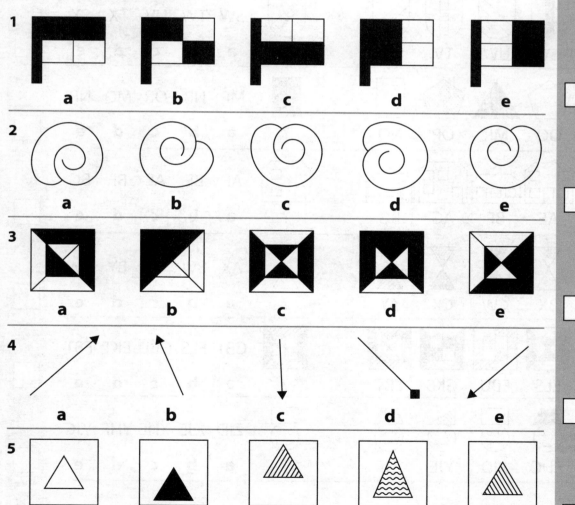

© Letts Educational Ltd, *an imprint of HarperCollins Publishers*

Mark

Non-verbal reasoning test

Breaking codes

The four images on the left each have a code. Work out how the codes go with these images. Now find the correct code from the list on the right that matches the fifth image. Circle the letter under the code that you think is the correct answer.

Example

VN   XP   VP   WO

    ?   WP VO WN XO XN

        a   b   (c)   d   e

*The fifth shape has three black circles. The 'three circles' pattern has the letter code W. Black shading has the letter code N. The correct answer is **c**.*

Now have a go at these similar questions. Circle the letter under the code that you think is the correct answer.

6

  SV   UW   TV   UX

   ?   SW TW UV TX SX

        a   b   c   d   e

7

  OQ   MR   OP   NQ

   ?   MP NP OR MQ NR

        a   b   c   d   e

8

  AE   BF   AG   BG

   ?   AF BE AE BF BG

        a   b   c   d   e

9

  BX   CW   CX   AY

   ?   AX BW CY BY AW

        a   b   c   d   e

10

  ELS   FBU   GKS   EBT

   ?   GBT FLS GBU EKT FBT

        a   b   c   d   e

11

  ZHC   XID   YJE   ZJF

   ?   ZID XJE XHE YHF YJC

        a   b   c   d   e

Finding relationships

Mark

Look at the pair of images on the left, connected by an arrow. Work out how the two images go together. Now look at the third image, which is followed by another arrow. Work out which of the five images on the right completes the second pair in the same way as the first pair. Circle the letter under the image that you think is the correct answer.

Example

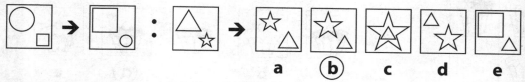

a   **(b)**   c   d   e

*The shapes swap position and size. The correct answer is **b**.*

Now have a go at these similar questions. Circle the letter under the image that you think is the correct answer.

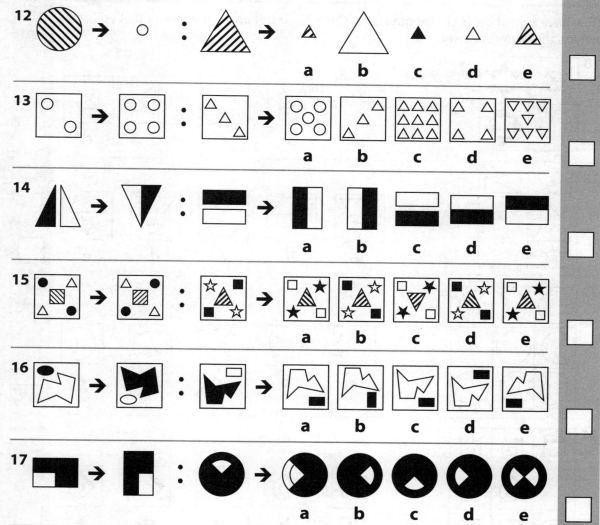

Non-verbal reasoning test

Non-verbal reasoning test

Spotting patterns

Mark

One of the boxes is missing from the grid on the left. Work out which of the five boxes on the right completes the grid. Circle the letter under the box that you think is the correct answer.

Example

  a   **b**   **c**   **d**   **e**

*As the images in the boxes move from left to right, the top section becomes black and a circle is added to the top. As the images in the boxes move from top to bottom, the size is reduced. The correct answer is **d**.*

Now have a go at these similar questions. Circle the letter under the square that you think is the correct answer.

18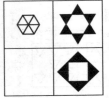

  a   **b**   **c**   **d**   **e**

19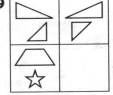

  a   **b**   **c**   **d**   **e**

20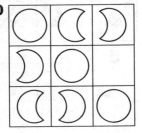

  a   **b**   **c**   **d**   **e**

21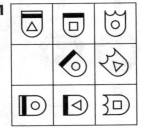

  a   **b**   **c**   **d**   **e**

Completing sequences

One of the boxes on the right completes the sequence or pattern on the left. Circle the letter under the box that you think is the correct answer.

Example

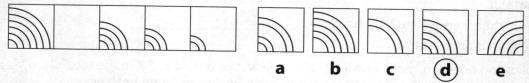

a   b   c   ⓓ   e

*As the sequence in the boxes moves from left to right, the number of curved lines is reduced by one each time; it is always the outer line that is removed. The correct answer is **d**.*

Now have a go at these similar questions. Circle the letter under the box that you think is the correct answer.

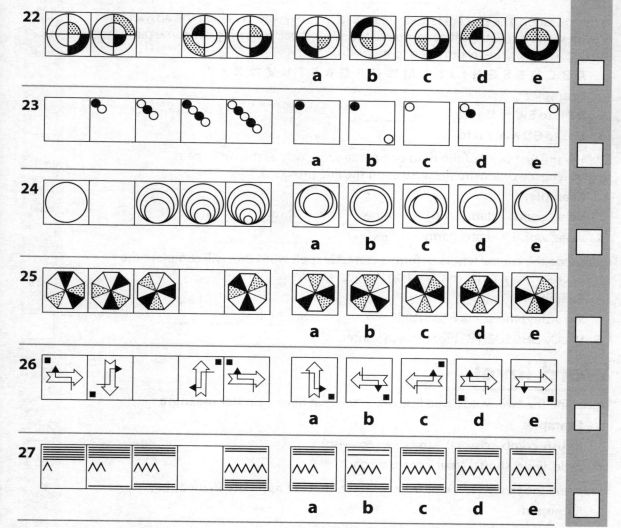

Non-verbal reasoning test

TEST ENDS

Letter level

Mark

In the following sentences, a word of **four letters** is hidden at the **end** of one word and the **start** of the next word. Write the hidden word on the lines provided, **using all the spaces you are given**. The letter order may **not** be changed.

Example:

The children we<u>re</u> <u>al</u>l late for school.   r e a l

1   Both islands are beautiful.   __ __ __ __

In the following question, move **one** letter from the first word and add it to the second word to make two new words. Do **not** rearrange any other letters. Write **both** new words, which **must make sense**, on the lines provided.

Example:

wash   pat   w a s _____   p a t h _____

2   link   sea   _____   _____

In this question, the pairs of letters are **linked** in some way. Write, on the answer line provided, the **two** letters that complete the second pair following the same pattern as the first. The alphabet is provided to help you.

A B C D E F G H I J K L M N O P Q R S T U V W X Y Z

Example:

DZ is to **EW** as **IS** is to   J P _____

3   **LI** is to **GD** as **BY** is to   _____

Change the first word of the third pair in the same way as the other pairs to give a new word. Write the answer on the line provided.

Example:

bone, bond   lane, land   mine,   m i n d _____

4   wore, worm   hare, harm   fire,   _____

Rearrange the capital letters to form a correctly spelt word that will complete the sentence sensibly. Write the word on the answer line.

Example:

We visited the science SMUUME.   M U S E U M _____

5   Prickly DHGSOEHEG hibernate in winter.   _____

Word level

Underline the **two** words, **one** from each set, that have a **similar meaning**.

Example:

(<u>brush</u>, comb, scissors)   (hair, <u>sweep</u>, wish)

6   (wild, wide, short)   (tall, broad, abroad)

Underline the **two** words, **one** from each set, that are **opposite in meaning**.

Example:

(<u>ancient</u>, crumbling, dusty)   (clean, <u>modern</u>, rich)

7   (borrow, barter, defend)   (purchase, lend, retrieve)

In the following questions, underline the **two** words, **one** from each set, that will complete each sentence in the most sensible way.

Example:

Seed is to (packet, <u>sow</u>, dig) as **bulb** is to (flower, light, <u>plant</u>).

8   **Mow** is to (lawn, tow, farmer) as **prune** is to (plum, tree, fruit).

In this question, the word in capitals has had a group of three letters taken out. These **three** letters spell another word, without rearranging the order. Write the **three-letter** word on the line provided. The sentence needs to make sense.

Example:

Kate was WING her favourite dress.   E A R _____

9   The old chair was UNSDY.   _____

In the following question, underline the **two** words that are **different** from the others.

Example:

car,   train,   <u>helicopter</u>,   <u>plane</u>,   lorry

10   cap,   coat,   skirt,   hat,   vest

Underline the **two** words, **one** from each set, that when put together, make **one** new, correctly spelt word. The order of the letters does not change. **The word from the set on the left always comes first**.

Example:

(van, <u>car</u>, wreck)   (<u>pet</u>, let, hold)

11   (paper, note, bag)   (book, shop, form)

Find **one** letter that will complete **both** pairs of words, finishing the first word and beginning the second word in each pair. The **same** letter must be used for both pairs of words. Write the letter on the lines provided.

Example:

va _n_ ot   pa _n_ ib

12   ru ____ ib   so ____ ar

Underline **one** word from the list in brackets that goes equally well with both pairs of words outside the brackets.

Example:

(elbow, divide, joint, <u>branch</u>, stump)   fork, split   limb, bough

13   (good, holiday, reasonable, fair, stall)   just, honest   carnival, fete

In the first set of three words, the middle word has been made from letters in the other two words. Complete the second set of words in the **same** way, to make the missing word, **which must make sense**. Write your answer on the line provided.

Example:

part (rat) top   calm (_lap_) pant

14   beam (barn) norm   gale (_____) even

Verbal reasoning test

Letter and number patterns

Mark

In the following question, letters stand for numbers. Work out the answer to the sum. Write your answer as a **letter** on the line provided.

Example:

If A = 2, B = 4, C = 5, D = 7, E = 10, what is the answer to this sum **written as a letter**?

B + C − A = __D__

15 If A = 3, B = 4, C = 6, D = 1, E = 9, what is the answer to this sum **written as a letter**?

A × B + D − B = _____

These **four** words have been written as **number codes**, but one of the codes is missing. The words and codes are not necessarily in the same order. Write the answer to the question on the line provided.

16 STEP   STOP   POST   PETS

          5138   **3865**   **5683**

Pick out the word with the number code 3815   _____

Find the next **pair of letters** in the series. The alphabet has been provided to help you.

A B C D E F G H I J K L M N O P Q R S T U V W X Y Z

Example:

AB   BC   CD   DE   EF   FG   __G H__

17 AD   BF   CH   DJ   EL   _____

The first code in the question has been solved for you. Use the **same** code to work out the second coded word. The alphabet will help you.

A B C D E F G H I J K L M N O P Q R S T U V W X Y Z

Example:

If the code for FIST is HKUV, what does HCP mean?   __F A N__

18 If the code for FOCUS is OXLDB, what is the code for SPACE?   _____

On the line, write the number that continues the sequence in the most sensible way.

Example:

4   8   13   19   26   __3 4_____

19 1   3   4   7   11   18   _____

Find the **relationship** between the **numbers** in the first two sets of brackets. The numbers in the third set of brackets are **related in the same way**. Find the missing number and add it to the final set of brackets.

Example:

(12 [2] 6)   (48 [6] 8)   (44 [__11__]4)

20 (9 [81] 9)   (7 [56] 8)   (6 [_____] 7)

Balance the **numbers** on each side of the equation. First, work out the calculation on the left. Next, find the missing number that will give the **same total** on the right-hand side.

Example:

(3 × 6) − 5 = (15 ÷ __3__) + 8

21 (3 + 8) − 2 = (4 × 5) − _____

22 Write the words into the grid so they can be read across or down.

Mark

Example:

PIP PAT
ACE ICE
PEN PEN

P	I	P
A	C	E
T	E	N

22 ORE BOA
ANT URN
NET BUN

Logic

23 Mark, Joe and Jess have gone out for pizza.

Mark always chooses a pepperoni pizza.

Joe and Jess share a large vegetarian pizza.

If these statements are true, only one of the sentences below must be true.

Which one? Underline the correct letter.

A Mark, Joe and Jess all like pizza more than any other food.

B Joe chose ham and pineapple pizza.

C The friends ordered two pizzas between them.

D Joe is vegetarian.

E Joe and Mark share a large pizza.

24 Anna, Billy, Gina and Ash are trying to organise a trip to the cinema but they are all very busy in the evenings.

Anna plays hockey on Mondays and visits her grandparents each Saturday evening.

Gina does drama on Thursdays and gymnastics on Tuesdays.

Billy does drama with Gina and plays football on Friday evening.

Ash plays in the same football team as Billy and goes fishing with his uncle all day each Sunday.

On which evening are all of the friends free to go to the cinema?

TEST ENDS

Choose a writing task from the following selection. Allow 45 minutes to complete this.

Fiction

1 Complete the story using the story opener…

The parcel was sitting on the doorstep humming quietly …

2 Write a story that ends with…

… although the view through the window was the same, everything had changed.

3 Write a scene from a play called 'It's not fair!'

Non-fiction

4 School uniform should be banned. Discuss.

5 Write a letter of complaint to the council about the leisure centre being closed at the weekend.

6 Explain how a new computer will improve your chances in life.

Mental maths answer sheet

Question	Answer	Jottings	Mark
1			
2			
3			
4			
5			
6			
7			
8			
9	$x =$		
10	£		
11			
12			
13	%		
14	%		
15			
16		3 4 7 8 19 21	
17			
18			
19	°		
20			
21			
22			
23			
24	mm		
25			

Follow the instructions on page 9 to give this test.

1   What is seventy-five rounded to the nearest ten?

2   Write in figures the number twenty thousand and nineteen.

3   Write all the factors of eighteen.

4   Find the total of seventy-four, sixteen and forty-one.

5   Subtract twenty-two from one hundred and ten.

6   Multiply forty-two by three.

7   Divide four hundred and ninety by seven.

8   Multiply the total of six and five by the square root of four.

9   If four x equals forty-eight, what is the value of x?

10   If forty-two pounds are shared equally between six friends, how much will each friend receive?

11   What is five divided by four as a mixed number?

12   Find the sum of two point two, three point three and four point four.

13   Write two-fifths as a percentage.

14   On Monday thirty-four percent of the school were absent. What percentage was present?

15   For every three green fish there are two red fish. If you have twelve green fish, how many red fish will there be?

16   Look at the numbers on your answer sheet: three, four, seven, eight, nineteen and twenty-one. What is the range of these numbers?

17   If you have five blue marbles and six green marbles in a bag, what is the probability of picking out a blue marble?

18   How many sides does a heptagon have?

19   How many degrees do the internal angles of a triangle add up to?

20   If one side of a regular hexagon is three centimetres long, what is its perimeter?

21   If one side of a square measures eight centimetres, what is the area?

22   What number is halfway between four point five and eleven point five?

23   What is half of seventeen kilograms?

24   What is thirty-two centimetres in millimetres?

25   How many days are there in February in a leap year?

Dictation

Your child should not read this passage before taking the test.

Read out the text slowly in short sections, leaving time for your child to write the text down.

Earthquake Island

The ground began to shake around midday when workers were at their desks, children were in the playground and people were generally going about their daily lives.

It was the first time in living memory that an earthquake had struck in daylight hours. However, all the island's inhabitants knew the emergency drill.

As buildings tumbled around them, the crowds gathered at the agreed meeting places. Despite the danger, there was little panic. 'It's really amazing!' commented one tourist, unfamiliar with the routine.

Spelling

Your child should not look at these words before taking the test.

Read out the words, repeating each word twice, and leaving time for your child to write it down.

A	cot	did	hen	jam	cup
	try	your	oil	blue	how
B	plum	pond	quest	blot	shaft
	forty	hearing	every	bought	wasp
C	like	shine	cube	shout	float
	daughter	plough	awkward	square	receipt
D	before	polite	neighbour	surprise	extreme
	disappear	pyramid	library	design	kitchen
E	chimney	environment	necessity	regulation	sergeant
	automatically	polystyrene	luminous	pictorial	expressive

The 11+ Maths test is often set as all multiple-choice questions, in a variety of formats. When going through practice papers it is important for your child to review the instruction text (this is usually at the top of a series of questions), before circling, underlining or filling in the answer.

The key instruction words are in bold in the following examples. Your child needs to get in the habit of looking out for these words before they answer questions.

Numbers and their properties

1 Find the two numbers that complete the sequence. **Underline** the two missing numbers *in the correct order*.

144, …, …, 81, 64, 49, 36

A 100, 121 **B** 42, 144 **C** 84, 99

D 121, 100 **E** 99, 84

Calculations

2 **Circle** the correct answer.

$7n - 4 = 52$ $n = \ldots$

A 8 **B** 11 **C** 56

D 28 **E** 59

Fractions, decimals and percentages

3 Sort these fractions, decimals and percentages in *order of size*, starting with the smallest. **Write** your answers on the **rules** provided.

$\frac{2}{3}$ 32% 0.23 $\frac{23}{46}$ 46% $\frac{9}{10}$

_____ _____ _____ _____ _____ _____

Working with charts and data

4 What is the probability of pulling a red fish from the tank?

A $\frac{3}{13}$ **B** $\frac{13}{4}$ **C** $\frac{5}{5}$

D $\frac{5}{13}$ **E** $\frac{13}{5}$

Choose the correct answer and **write** the letter in the **triangle** next to the fish tank.

Shape and space

5 If a rectangular swimming pool has a width of 15m and its overall perimeter is 90m, what is its length?

A 60 **B** 30 **C** 15 **D** 13 **E** 20

Write the letter of the correct answer in the **box**.

Measuring

6 If a clock reads 10.05 and it is 15 minutes fast, what is the actual time? **Write** the answer on the **line** provided.

_____

Making connections

'Making connections' is the first process in learning about non-verbal reasoning and involves comparing images to find relationships. In some questions there may be more than one relationship and the ability to identify these and establish which are relevant are important skills.

This example shows a typical question on making connections.

Example

Look at the five shapes in each row. Work out what connects *four* of the shapes and makes the other shape the odd one out. Which shape is most *unlike* the others. Circle the letter under the shape most *unlike* the others.

 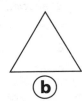

    a   **ⓑ**   **c**   **d**   **e**

Shapes a, c, d and e all have four sides; shape b has three sides. The shape most unlike the others is **b**.

Common connections

These questions test the ability to find similarities and progressive changes, using a sound knowledge *of shape, rotation and sequence.*

Important skills in finding common connections in shapes include identifying…

- different styles of line such as thin and thick solid lines, dashed and dotted lines
- regular and irregular shapes
- solid and outlined shapes
- patterns such as spots, grids, diagonal and vertical stripes
- enlargements and reductions.

Connection of direction, angle and symmetry

These questions test the ability to find similarities and progressive changes, using a sound knowledge of *direction, translation, rotation* and *sequence.*

Important skills in finding common connections with arrows, angles and symmetry include identifying…

- different styles of arrow heads such as solid, outlined, lines, diamonds
- different styles of arrow tails such as one, two and three tail fins
- the direction of arrows
- different types of angles such as right angle, obtuse angle, acute angle
- shapes and patterns with lines of symmetry.

  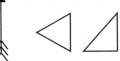 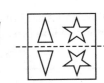

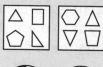

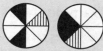

Finding similarities and differences

More complex connection questions require the ability to find differences in shapes and patterns as well as similarities.

A key skill in tackling questions on similarities and differences is the ability to spot differences between…

- simple shapes
- small groups of shapes
- segmented shapes such as shaded fractions
- compound shapes such as the car on the right.

Spotting distractions

Being able to identify all elements in a problem and then pick out those that are used for distraction (and therefore not relevant) are the skills needed in higher-level questions.

Practice in working with 'distraction' questions should include reviewing…

- each element in a question, one at a time
- the question as a whole, to look for overall patterns and identify similarities and differences.

Look at the two shapes on the left in this example. Decide what makes them similar to each other. Now find the shape on the right that is most like the two shapes on the left.

                       a   **b**   **c**   **d**   **e**

The shading is a distraction because it varies from picture to picture. Only c is a regular shape, so this is the correct answer.

SKILLS TESTER

1 Look at the five shapes in the row below. What connects *four* of the shapes and makes the other shape the odd one out? Circle the letter under the shape that you think is most *unlike* the others.

      a   **b**   **c**   **d**   **e**

2 Look at the two shapes on the left. Decide what makes these two shapes *similar* to each other. Now find the shape on the right that is *most like* the two shapes on the left. Circle the letter under the shape that you think is the correct answer.

                           a   **b**   **c**   **d**   **e**

'Breaking codes' questions introduce the dimension of using letters to represent features within the images being studied. These questions require two steps to reach the solution: comparing the images to work out the code and applying these findings to other images to check the relationships.

This example shows a typical question on breaking codes.

The four shapes on the left each have a code. Work out how the codes go with these shapes. Now find the correct code from the list on the right that matches the fifth shape.

Example

Circle the letter under the code that you think is the correct answer.

*The fifth shape is a **circle** and has a **hatched pattern**.*

*A circle has the letter code L. A hatched pattern has the letter code T. The answer is **b**.*

Codes with two letters

Before beginning questions on codes with two letters, it is important to understand that each letter links to a feature in the images.

Skills needed in breaking the codes are…

- spotting codes with common letters (such as KR, KT) and checking the images for similarities
- identifying changes in…
  - shape
  - size
  - shading and pattern
  - number
  - orientation
  - groups of shapes
- reviewing the letters and features to confirm any findings
- applying the logic to other images
- eliminating and confirming possible codes for the remaining images.

In simpler codes, everything in the image changes, such as in the shaded shapes below.

In more complex codes, one part of the image changes, as in this example. The arrowheads and direction change, the tail fins stay the same and act as a distractor.

Codes with three letters

The key skill in solving problems involving codes with three letters is the ability to work through problems in a logical sequence.

Skills needed in breaking codes with three letters are…

- spotting codes with common letters such as DLT, DKR, and checking the images for similarities, as shown below
- identifying changes in…
  - shape
  - size
  - shading and pattern
  - number
  - orientation
  - groups of shapes
  - reflection

- reviewing the letters and features to confirm any findings
- attempting to work out what the other letters in the code stand for
- applying the logic to other images
- eliminating and confirming possible codes for remaining images.

These more complex codes always involve a number of steps to break them.

In the example below, the four shapes on the left each have a code. Work out how the codes go with the images. Work out the code that matches the fifth shape.

| DLT | CJR | DKR | BJS | ? |

The answer is CKR: C is the pattern of two segmented circles that don't line up with each other, K is the black and white outer segment, R is the white chequered inner segment.

SKILLS-TESTER

The four images on the left each have a code. Work out how the codes go with these images.

Now find the correct code from the list on the right that matches the fifth image.

Circle the letter under the code that you think is the correct answer.

1

QX	RY	PW	QY	?	PX	QW	RX	PY	RW
					a	b	c	d	e

2

CAG	CBF	DAG	EAH	?	EBF	DBG	EAG	CBH	DAH
					a	b	c	d	e

'Finding relationships' questions test your child's ability to identify 'common connections' to solve problems.

This example shows a typical question on finding relationships.

Example

Look at the two images on the left, connected by an arrow. Work out how the two images go together. Now look at the third image, which is followed by another arrow. Work out which of the five images on the right completes the second pair in the same way as the first pair. Circle the letter under the image that you think is the correct answer.

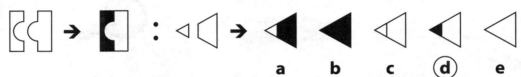

*Image 2 is formed by joining the two shapes in image 1 together, and shading the first section black. The correct answer is **d**.*

Changing shapes

An awareness of the elements that can change in pairs of images is key to tackling questions where the relationships involve shapes.

These questions need skills in identifying…

- the type of shape
- the position of the shapes
- the size of the shapes
- the number of shapes
- how the shapes are filled
- how all the elements work together.

Number and proportion

Working through problems involving 'number and proportion' requires skills in comparing the number of elements within the pairs of images.

Skills needed to tackle number and proportion questions are…

- counting different elements within an image and comparing constants
- spotting increasing and decreasing sequences, such as in angles and sides

- discounting elements as a result of these comparisons
- identifying what fraction or proportion of an image is shaded or patterned.

Moving and connecting shapes

The primary skills needed in moving and connecting shapes are rotation, reflection and translation.

To tackle 'moving and connecting shapes' questions, the skills needed are…

- identifying shapes within a given area and their position in relation to each other
- identifying constants in a pair of images: which shapes stay the same shape, size and position and which shapes change
- spotting rotations and reflections and the patterns that can be made following these processes
- identifying distractors in resulting patterns
- visualising how irregular shapes can fit together.

Finding relationships

Reflecting shapes

An understanding of the mirror line is the key skill in working with questions on reflecting shapes, as this indicates exactly where the image is to be reflected.

Using tracing paper when working on these questions can build skills quickly.

Skills needed when reflecting shapes are…

- identifying that a reflected image is being used

- identifying whether a single shape or a group of shapes is being reflected

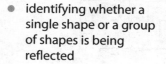

- checking the positioning of the mirror line, e.g. whether it should be vertical, horizontal or diagonal.

Some reflections are simple to spot but others are frequently confused with rotations.

Rotating shapes

Questions on rotating shapes assume a knowledge of angles, anticlockwise and clockwise.

Skills needed when working with questions involving rotation are…

- identifying that the shape or shapes have been rotated

- identifying the point of rotation

- applying the concept of *degree of rotation* in 45° steps, i.e. 45°, 90°, 135°, 180°, 225°, 270°, 315°.

- spotting where segments within an image are rotated. For complex images, there may be both clockwise and anticlockwise rotations, like this.

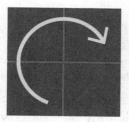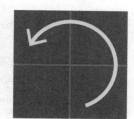

SKILLS TESTER

1 There are two similar boxes on the left. Work out which of the five boxes on the right is most like the first two. Circle the letter under the box that you think is the correct answer.

                                         a   **b**   **c**   **d**   **e**

2 Look at the pair of images on the left, connected by an arrow. Work out how the two images relate to each other. Now look at the third image, which is followed by another arrow. Work out which of the five images on the right completes the second pair in the same way as the first pair. Circle the letter under the image that you think is the correct answer.

 → : →

                                         a   **b**   **c**   **d**   **e**

Spotting patterns

'Spotting patterns' when working with grids requires a combination of the skills previously explained in this chapter, as at least two changes are included in every question. Having identified the relationships between the boxes on the grid, a series of options are provided to complete the empty box.

This example shows a typical question on spotting patterns.

Example

One of the boxes is missing from the grid on the left. Work out which of the five boxes on the right completes the grid. Circle the letter under the box that you think is the correct answer.

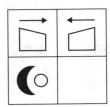

a   b   c   d   e

*The images in the boxes in the left-hand column are reflected vertically. The correct answer is **b**.*

2 × 2 grids

Understanding that images can change across rows and down columns in the grid is important when answering questions involving 2 × 2 grids.

Skills needed to solve 2 × 2 grid problems are…

- working methodically across rows and down columns to spot patterns
- identifying changes in size
- identifying changes in shape
- identifying changes in shading
- spotting changes in the number of shapes
- tracking rotations
- visualising reflections
- counting numbers of sides or angles.

This example illustrates changes in shape and size.

   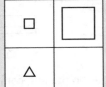

Some questions will include even more elements. This example contains reflections, colour changes and shape changes.

a   b   c   d   e

3 × 3 grids

Following a number of steps and identifying distractions make answering problems with 3 × 3 grids more challenging.

Skills needed to solve 3 × 3 grid problems are…

- working methodically across rows and down columns to spot patterns
- identifying changes in size
- identifying changes in shading
- spotting changes in the number of shapes
- tracking rotations
- visualising reflections
- counting numbers of sides or angles.

This example shows the reflected patterns coloured in so that they can be visualised more easily.

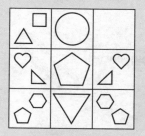  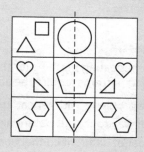

SKILLS TESTER

One of the boxes is missing from the grid on the left. Work out which of the five boxes on the right completes the grid. Circle the letter under the box that you think is the correct answer.

1

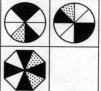 

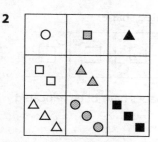

   a   **b**   **c**   **d**   **e**

2

   a   **b**   **c**   **d**   **e**

The mathematical principles behind finding number sequences apply in exactly the same way to non-verbal reasoning sequences. The ability to spot a progressive sequence or 'story' through a series of images is the targeted skill.

This example shows a typical question on completing sequences.

Example

One of the boxes on the right completes the sequence or pattern on the left.
Circle the letter under the box that you think is the correct answer.

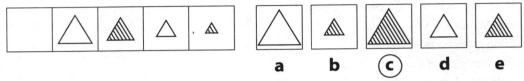

The triangle decreases in size each time and alternates between being striped and clear.
*The correct answer is **c**.*

Repeating patterns

All sequences include repeating patterns (or they could not be defined as sequences).
Questions on repeating patterns require the ability to spot these changes.

Skills needed to solve problems with repeating patterns are…

- working in a linear way to try out potential links
- reviewing a number of different connections to identify patterns
- building up a picture of the sequence
- predicting the pattern both forwards and backwards to check answers
- checking that all the criteria have been satisfied
- identifying changes in number, line style, angles, shape, shading, reflection and rotation.

One-step patterns

'One-step patterns' test a basic ability to work with sequences that show just one change at a time.

Skills needed to solve one-step patterns are…

- identifying a simple, progressive sequence

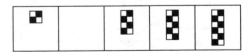

- deconstructing a sequence if a pattern is reversed

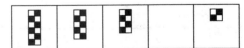

- picking out a rotated shape

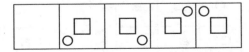

- spotting when shapes have been relocated within a series.

Completing sequences

Two-step patterns

'Two-step patterns' have two changeable elements that need to be identified and followed.

Skills needed to solve two-step patterns are...

- isolating all elements of one sequence and reviewing its validity before moving on to the next

- working with two patterns simultaneously

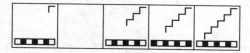

- identifying two overlapping repeating patterns

- deconstructing sequences if patterns are reversed.

Number patterns

Number patterns in non-verbal reasoning use visual images to represent numerical sequences involving the four operations (+ − × ÷) and common number patterns. Division is rarely used (with powers of two being the most common) and the answers are always whole numbers.

The following skills are essential when working with problems involving number patterns:

- addition and subtraction of whole numbers

- multiplication and division of whole numbers

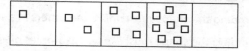

- square numbers to 100

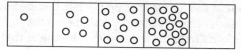

- prime numbers
- triangular numbers.

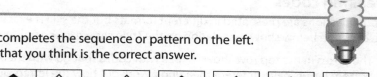

SKILLS TESTER

One of the boxes on the right completes the sequence or pattern on the left. Circle the letter under the box that you think is the correct answer.

1

   a   b   c   d   e

2

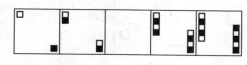

   a   b   c   d   e

Question types

The 11+ Non-verbal reasoning questions are typically multiple-choice and are presented in a range of formats.

Although the instructions often specify that the answers should be circled or filled in on a separate sheet, the instructions may vary. All answers must be marked as instructed or the marks may not be awarded, even if the correct option is chosen.

This section gives some typical variations in answer style.

Making connections

These questions include two different formats:

A Finding the shape *most unlike* the others in a set.

B Finding the shape *most like* two examples given.

This question shows the second, more complex version.

1 Look at the two shapes on the left. Decide what makes these two shapes *similar* to each other. Now find the shape on the right that is *most like* the two shapes on the left. **Circle** the letter under the shape that you think is the correct answer.

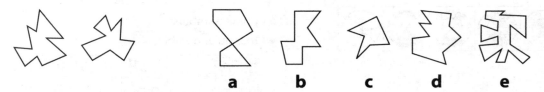

a   b   c   d   e

Breaking codes

These questions are presented in different formats but the skill is exactly the same. The question below shows a variation on the style shown in the pull-out practice test.

2 The boxes in the top row show shapes with codes that go with them. The top and bottom letters have different meanings. Work out how the letters go with the shapes and then find the correct code for the shape in the bottom row. **Write** the answers in the spaces provided in the box.

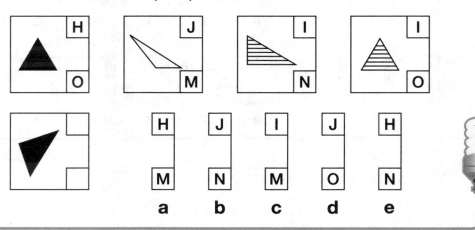

a   b   c   d   e

Finding relationships

These questions can follow two different formats.

A The simpler style has two images with similarities that should be matched from a selection given.

B The second, more common, style involves completing a new pair of images following a given pattern. This style is shown below.

3 Look at the two images on the left, connected by an arrow. Work out how the two shapes relate to each other. Now look at the third image, which is followed by another arrow. Work out which of the five images on the right completes the second pair in the same way as the first pair. **Write** the letter for the correct answer on the line provided.

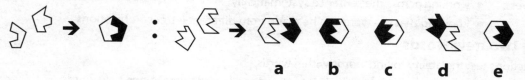

                                    a   **b**   **c**   **d**   **e**

Spotting patterns

These questions all follow the same format, with the difference being the complexity of the grid. Some questions involve completing a 2 x 2 grid and others a 3 x 3 grid. However, the style of questions is laid out in the same way.

4 One of the boxes is missing from the grid on the left. Work out which of the five boxes on the right completes the grid. **Circle** the letter under the box that you think is the correct answer.

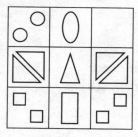

                            a   **b**   **c**   **d**   **e**

Completing sequences

These questions all follow the same format, although sometimes the incomplete sequence is separated from the answer options by a line. Usually, a range of options is given to choose from but trying to draw the answer may also help in completing the sequence.

5 One of the boxes in this sequence is missing. **Draw** in the missing image.

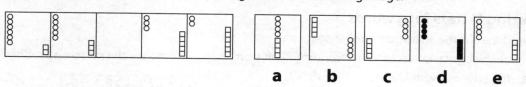

                                    a   **b**   **c**   **d**   **e**

Letter level

The simplest types of verbal reasoning question involve working with small groups of letters to make words or patterns. The questions test your child's ability to work with and analyse the structure of words and the alphabet.

Making words across a gap

These questions test the ability to work logically by looking closely at the beginnings and endings of words in a sentence.

1 In the following sentence, a word of four letters is hidden at the end of one word and the start of the next word. The letter order may not be changed.

Example: The elephant walked slowly through the grass. __ __ __ __

This involves… ● working across the sentence systematically
             ● knowing that the word can be made from different letter combinations.

Making two new words

These questions test the ability to find words within words.

2 Move one letter from the first word and add it to the second word to make two new words. Do not rearrange any other letters.

Example: chat   tick   _____   _____

This involves… ● removing letters from the first word to find possible new words
             ● listing the possible letters
             ● trying out these letter options in the second word in a systematic way.

Analogies with letter changes

These questions test the ability to count and position letters within the alphabet.

3 In the example, the pairs of letters are linked in some way. Find the two letters that complete the second pair, following the same pattern as the two pairs on the left.

     A B C D E F G H I J K L M N O P Q R S T U V W X Y Z

Example: **BF** is to **CE** as **GK** is to _____

This involves… ● comparing the position within the alphabet of letter 1 in each pair
             ● comparing the position within the alphabet of letter 2 within each pair
             ● transferring the pattern to the uncompleted pair.

Complete the third pair

These questions test the ability to identify and apply a pattern of letter change.

4 Change the first word of the third pair in the same way as the other pairs to give a new word.

Example: part, spar   cart, scar   tart, _____

This involves… ● looking for the pattern of change in the letters in the first pair of words
             ● trying out the pattern in the second pair
             ● applying the pattern to the uncompleted pair.

Reordering letters into words

These questions test the ability to decipher anagrams.

5 Rearrange the capital letters to form a correctly spelt word that will complete the sentence sensibly.

Example: The scientist went back to
          the BARLOARYOT   _____

This involves… ● predicting possible words
             ● rearranging letters to test the predictions.

SKILLS TESTER

Complete the examples in the explanations.

An understanding of word meaning, and how words are constructed and connected in sentences are the English skills that help children to solve problems at 'Word level' in verbal reasoning.

Closest in meaning

These questions test the ability to pick out synonyms.

1   Pick out one word from each set with a similar meaning.

Example: (tea, coffee, cup) (plate, mug, fork)

This involves…   • taking one word at a time from the first bracket and assessing it in relation to each word in the second bracket in turn
   • recognising word types.

Different in meaning

These questions test the ability to pick out antonyms.

2   Pick out one word from each set that are opposite in meaning.

Example: (hushed, loud, hammer)   (happy, quiet, sad)

This involves…   • taking one word at a time from the first bracket and assessing it in relation to each word in the second bracket in turn
   • recognising word types.

Analogies by word meaning

These questions test the ability to find relationships between words and apply them in new situations.

3   Pick out one word from each set to complete the sentence in a sensible way.

Example: Moon is to (night, stars, light) as **Sun** is to (seaside, sunny, day).

This involves…   • identifying possible relationships
   • sorting and discounting choices
   • checking and concluding.

Incomplete words

These questions test the ability to understand word formation and spelling.

4   The word in capitals has had a group of three letters taken out. These three letters make a word, without rearranging the order. Rewrite the sentence, inserting the word in the correct place. The sentence must make sense.

Example: The boy SPED on the wet mud.

This involves…   • looking at the text for clues to the possible word
   • considering different word types
   • testing three-letter words that could be inserted
   • working systematically through the word with a range of options.

Odd one out

These questions test the ability to identify associations between words.

5   Pick out two words from this group that are different from the others.

Example: button, jumper, zip, trousers, toggle

This involves…   • looking for themes and categorising similarities and differences
   • discounting common themes to find the solution.

Word level

Compound words

These questions test the ability to identify prefixes and suffixes and create compound words.

6 Pick out one word from each set that when put together make one new, correctly spelt word. The order of the letters does not change. The word always begins with the word on the left.

Example: (below, under, way)   (walk, run, stand)

This involves…   ● taking one word at a time from the first bracket and assessing it in relation to each word in the second bracket, in turn
        ● recognising compound words
        ● understanding how to order prefixes and suffixes.

Word pairings

These questions test the ability to work methodically using the alphabet and spelling patterns.

7 Find one letter that will complete both pairs of words, finishing the first word and beginning the second word in each pair. *The same letter must be used for both pairs of words.*

Example: st ____ et   sk ____ es

This involves…   ● identifying possible letters for the first pair of words
        ● trying these possibilities out with the second pair to reach a conclusion.

Double meanings

These questions test the ability to connect verbs and nouns.

8 Pick out one word from the list in brackets that goes equally well with both pairs of words outside the brackets.

Example: (lift, drive, bear, polar, crossing)   mongoose, fox   transport, carry

This involves…   ● taking one word at a time from the brackets and assessing it in relation to each pair of words in turn
        ● recognising word types and double meanings
        ● trying out alternative meanings with each word pair.

Word creation

These questions test the ability to order letters following a given pattern.

9 In the first set of three words, the middle word has been made from a *set pattern* of letters from the other two words. Complete the second set of words in the same way to make the missing word. A completed answer has been given to help you.

Example: park (rat) top   calm (*lap*) pant

                 post (past) lack   most (_____) lick

This involves…   ● numbering the letters of the two external words in order. For example,

        p a r k   *(r a t)*   *t o p*   *c a l m* *(l a p)* *p a n t*
        1 2 3 4   *3 2 5*   *5 6 7*   *1 2 3 4*   *3 2 5*   *5 6 7 8*

        ● trying out different combinations when a letter is common to both external words.

SKILLS TESTER

Complete the examples in the explanations.

'Letter and number patterns' questions involve working methodically with complex sequences and relationships.

Letters with number codes

These questions test the ability to carry out precise substitutions using abstract concepts.

1 Letters stand for numbers in the following sum. Work out the answers for each sum and *write the answer as a letter.*

Example: If A = 2, B = 4, C = 6, D = 8 and E = 10

A × C – D = _____

This involves…
- writing the number value under each letter in the equation
- calculating accurately in the correct order
- linking the answer to the corresponding letter.

Words with number codes

These questions test the ability to spot identifiable patterns within words.

2 These four words have been written as number codes. One of the codes is missing. The words and codes are not necessarily in the same order.

Example: SAND   BAND   SOON   BOND

2334   5346   2146

Pick out the word with the number code 5146.

This involves…
- looking for words with common patterns, e.g. words beginning with the same letter
- using these patterns and applying logic to decipher the other codes.

Alphabet pair sequences

These questions test the ability to count and position letters within the alphabet, then to apply this logic to predict other letters in the sequence.

3 Find the missing pairs of letters in the series. Use the alphabet to help you.

A B C D E F G H I J K L M N O P Q R S T U V W X Y Z

Example: AZ BY CX _____   EV FU _____

This involves…
- comparing the position within the alphabet of letter 1 in each pair
- comparing the position within the alphabet of letter 2 within each pair
- transferring the pattern to missing pairs in the sequence.

Letter codes

These questions test the ability to find relationships between letters, using three separate sets of data, to solve codes.

4 The word in capitals is written in code. Use this information to decipher the second word written in the same code. Use the alphabet to help you.

A B C D E F G H I J K L M N O P Q R S T U V W X Y Z

Example: The code for HOST is GNRS. What does OQHL stand for?

This involves…
- keying in the initial word to the alphabet
- counting on or back to discover the position of the code letters
- applying this information to change either code letters to words, or words to code letters.

Number sequences

These questions test the ability to analyse number sequences using the four operations.

5 Find the number that continues the sequence in the most sensible way.

Example: 2   4   8   16   32   _____

This involves…
- looking at patterns in the gaps between the numbers
- observing where patterns repeat, extend or alternate
- applying a pattern to solve the problem.

Letter and number patterns

Number patterns and equations

These questions test the ability to identify the use of the four operations and to balance equations.

6 Find the relationship between the numbers in the first two sets of brackets. The numbers in the third set are related in the same way. Find the missing number and add it to the set of brackets.

Example 1:   (31[25]6)   (19[12]7)   (21[____]8)

This involves… ● testing each operation against the outer numbers in the first bracket
  ● applying these findings to the second bracket to check findings
  ● using conclusions to complete the calculation in the third set of brackets.

7 Balance the numbers on each side of the equation. Start by working out the calculation on the left. Next, find the missing number that will give the same total on the right-hand side.

Example 2: $(3 \times 3) + 5 = ($ ____ $\div 2) + 2$

This involves… ● solving the left-hand side of the equation
  ● applying the inverse operation to calculate the answer
  ● checking that the equation balances.

3 × 3 grids

These questions test the ability to spot common relationships between consonants and vowels within words.

8 Write the words in the grid so that they can be read across or down.

Example: SIR, ARE, WED, SAW, IRE, RED

This involves… ● looking for words with consonants as the second letter to try out across the centre of the grid
  ● trying out words in the cross formation
  ● positioning other words to fit through trial and error.

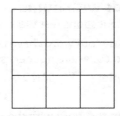

SKILLS TESTER

Complete the examples in the explanations.

Logic

The two question types in this section require the application of logic to problems in several stages.

SKILLS TESTER

Complete the examples in the explanations.

True statement

These questions test the ability to break information into parts and check against the facts given.

1 James is taller than Peter but shorter than the twins, Inez and Pedro, who are the same height.

If the above statement is true, only one of the sentences below must be true. Which one? Underline the correct letter.

  A Peter is taller than Pedro.

  B The twins are shorter than James.

  C Inez and Peter are the same height.

  D Peter is the shortest.

This involves…

● taking one statement at a time and creating notes or diagrams as appropriate to organise the information

● checking each statement against assumptions made to reach a conclusion.

Deduction

These questions test the ability to take a set of statements and make a deduction from the information given.

2 Jennifer left school at 3.30pm. It took her 10 minutes to walk to the shop. She bought some sweets and an ice-cream, then left the shop 13 minutes later and walked home, just in time for her favourite programme at 4.45pm.

How long did it take Jennifer to get from the shop to her house?

This involves…

● taking one statement at a time and creating notes or diagrams as appropriate to organise the information

● making a deduction from the information given.

The 11+ Verbal reasoning questions are sometimes multiple-choice and are presented in a range of formats, as you have seen in this section.

Although the instructions often specify that the answers should be circled or filled in on a separate sheet, the instructions may vary. All answers must be marked as instructed or the marks may not be awarded, even if the correct option is chosen. This section gives some typical variations in answer style.

Letter level

There is sometimes variation within a question type and this can be distracting when encountering a problem in an unexpected form. In these instances it can be helpful to look for skills that are familiar. The example below shows possible variations in questions about reordering letters into words.

A Finding anagrams to make sense in a sentence.

1 Rearrange the capital letters to form a correctly spelt word that will complete the sentence sensibly. **Write** the answer on the line.

The student packed his EATUSICS for his trip abroad. _____

B Finding words that can or cannot be made from a given word.

2 **Underline** the word that cannot be made from the word in capitals.

ENTERTAINMENT   retain   trainer

meant   matter

Both questions involve exactly the same skill in reordering letters.

Word level

There is a wide variety of Word level question types. Most involve comparing the meaning of words or matching or moving letters to make a new word. The instructions on how to answer each question may vary.

3 **Circle** one word from each set that when put together make one new, correctly spelt word. The order of the letters does not change. The word always begins with the word on the left in the first set of brackets.

(through, thorough, bred)

(unkind, wicked, fare)

Letter and number patterns

In some problems, a single piece of information is provided with which to answer a number of questions, as in this example of a Words with number codes problem.

Three of these four words have been written as number codes. One of the codes is missing. The words and codes are not necessarily in the same order. Work out the answers to these questions and write the answers on the rules provided.

SOLD   LOAD   LOOK   SOAK
3226   1234   1256

4 What is the missing code? _____

5 What is the code for SOAK? _____

Logic

Logic questions involve working out the answer in a series of steps. There are often distractions put in to mislead, so checking the answer is important.

6 Charlotte, Matthew and Chrissy all have to be in bed by 9pm on a school night. Matthew gets tired easily and is always in bed by 8.50pm. On Thursday night, Chrissy's bus home from Guides broke down and she didn't arrive home till 9.15pm.

If these statements are true, only one of the sentences below must be true. Which one? Write the letter representing the correct answer on the line provided.

A Charlotte sometimes goes to bed late.

B Chrissy is never in bed on time.

C Matthew is never late for bed on a school night.

D Chrissy is sometimes in bed by 8.30pm.

E Matthew sometimes misses his bus home.

_____

3 Reviewing your child's skills: 11+ essentials

The 11+ Essentials pages are provided as a summary of some key facts your child may find useful in the 11+ tests.

Confusable words

There are many words in the English language that sound the same or similar, but are spelt differently and have different meanings. The selection below shows some of the words that are most commonly confused.

Accept	To agree to take something. *Example: Sarah accepted the surprise gift.*
Except	Not including. *Example: All the parts of the model were there except for the legs.*
Advice	A suggestion about how to do something. *Example: Andy was not happy with the advice Dad had given him.*
Advise	To suggest something. *Example: I advise you not to do it!*
Allowed	The past tense of the verb 'to allow'. *Example: I was allowed to stay up late.*
Aloud	When a thought is spoken. *Example: Jenny was reading aloud to her brother.*
Cereal	Something eaten for breakfast. *Example: Tammy ate a large bowl of cereal.*
Serial	A long-running programme; a series of events. *Example: The popular serial won 10 awards at the ceremony.*
Coarse	Rough. *Example: The sandpaper was very coarse.*
Course	A study programme, part of a meal. *Example: Anwar signed up for the maths revision course.*
Desert	A dry, sandy landscape. *Example: They rode camels across the desert.*
Dessert	A pudding. *Example: We ate chocolate cake for dessert!*
Hair	The noun to describe animal or human hair. *Example: He brushed his hair.*
Hare	The noun to describe a large rabbit-like animal. *Example: The hare ran across the field.*
It's	Short for 'it is' *Example: It's a long way home.*
Its	Belonging to it – no apostrophe! *Example: She stroked its head.*
Loose	Unfastened or released. *Example: He opened the box to let the bird loose.*
Lose	To mislay something. *Example: They knew it was precious and didn't want to lose it.*

Sight	The ability to see. *Example: Anne's new glasses improved her sight.*
Site	A location or place. *Example: It was an excellent site for their tent!*
Their	Belonging to them. *Example: They read their books.*
Theirs	Belonging to them (it is theirs) – no apostrophe! *Example: The books were theirs.*
There	A place. *Example: He sat over there.*
There's	Short for 'there is'. *Example: There's a fly in my soup!*
They're	Short for 'they are'. *Example: They're reading aloud.*
To	The start of a verb. *Example: To jump.*
Too	Also or excessive. *Example: They came along too. There were too many rabbits.*
Two	The number 2. *Example: There were two elephants.*
Weather	The climate. *Example: Bad weather was expected.*
Whether	Introducing an alternative. *Example: I didn't know whether to buy a chocolate bar or an ice-cream.*
Wear	To put clothing on. *Example: Can I wear your scarf?*
We're	Short for 'we are'. *Example: We're going on holiday to Spain.*
Were	The past tense of 'to be'. *Example: Ahmed and Jamil were reading the newspaper.*
Where	The location of something. *Example: Where did I put my MP3 player?*
Who's	Short for 'who is'. *Example: Who's sleeping in my bed?*
Whose	Belonging to 'whom'. *Example: Whose book is this?*

Factors of numbers to 100

The number 1 and the number itself has been omitted from this list. Numbers greater than 1 that are not featured here are prime numbers.

Number	Factors
4	2
6	2, 3
8	2, 4
9	3
10	2, 5
12	2, 3, 4, 6
14	2, 7
15	3, 5
16	2, 4, 8
18	2, 3, 6, 9
20	2, 4, 5, 10
21	3, 7
22	2, 11
24	2, 3, 4, 6, 8, 12
25	5
26	2, 13
27	3, 9
28	2, 4, 7, 14
30	2, 3, 5, 6, 10, 15
32	2, 4, 8, 16
33	3, 11
34	2, 17
35	5, 7
36	2, 3, 4, 6, 9, 12, 18
38	2, 19
39	3, 13
40	2, 4, 5, 8, 10, 20
42	2, 3, 6, 7, 14, 21
44	2, 4, 11, 22
45	3, 5, 9, 15
46	2, 23
48	2, 3, 4, 6, 8, 12, 16, 24
49	7
50	2, 5, 10, 25
51	3, 17
52	2, 4, 13, 26
54	2, 3, 6, 9, 18, 27

Number	Factors
55	5, 11
56	2, 4, 7, 8, 14, 28
57	3, 19
58	2, 29
60	2, 3, 4, 5, 6, 10, 12, 15, 20, 30
62	2, 31
63	3, 7, 9, 21
64	2, 4, 8, 16, 32
65	5, 13
66	2, 3, 6, 11, 22, 33
68	2, 4, 17, 34
69	3, 23
70	2, 5, 7, 10, 14, 35
72	2, 3, 4, 6, 8, 9, 12, 18, 24, 36
74	2, 37
75	3, 5, 15, 25
76	2, 4, 19, 38
77	7, 11
78	2, 3, 6, 13, 26, 39
80	2, 4, 5, 8, 10, 16, 20, 40
81	3, 9, 27
82	2, 41
84	2, 3, 4, 6, 7, 12, 14, 21, 28, 42
85	5, 17
86	2, 43
87	3, 29
88	2, 4, 8, 11, 22, 44
90	2, 3, 5, 6, 9, 10, 15, 18, 30, 45
91	7, 13
92	2, 4, 23, 46
93	3, 31
94	2, 47
95	5, 19
96	2, 3, 4, 6, 8, 12, 16, 24, 32, 48
98	2, 7, 14, 49
99	3, 9, 11, 33
100	2, 4, 5, 10, 20, 25, 50

Square numbers

$1 \times 1 = 1 \qquad 1^2$

$2 \times 2 = 4 \qquad 2^2$

$3 \times 3 = 9 \qquad 3^2$

$4 \times 4 = 16 \qquad 4^2$

$5 \times 5 = 25 \qquad 5^2$

$6 \times 6 = 36 \qquad 6^2$

$7 \times 7 = 49 \qquad 7^2$

$8 \times 8 = 64 \qquad 8^2$

$9 \times 9 = 81 \qquad 9^2$

Triangular numbers

1 ●

3 ● ●

6 ● ● ●

10 ● ● ● ●

15 ● ● ● ● ●

21 ● ● ● ● ● ●

28 ● ● ● ● ● ● ●

36 ● ● ● ● ● ● ● ●

Prime numbers to 409

2	3	5	7
11	13	17	19
23	29	31	37
41	43	47	53
59	61	67	71
73	79	83	89
97	101	103	107
109	113	127	131
137	139	149	151
157	163	167	173
179	181	191	193
197	199	211	223
227	229	233	239
241	251	257	263
269	271	277	281
283	293	307	311
313	317	331	337
347	349	353	359
367	373	379	383
389	397	401	409

3 Reviewing your child's skills: 11+ essentials

Place value

tens of thousands (TTh)	thousands (Th)	hundreds (H)	tens (T)	units/ones (U)	tenths (t)	hundredths (h)	thousandths (th)
90 000	9000	900	90	9	0.9	0.09	0.009
80 000	8000	800	80	8	0.8	0.08	0.008
70 000	7000	700	70	7	0.7	0.07	0.007
60 000	6000	600	60	6	0.6	0.06	0.006
50 000	5000	500	50	5	0.5	0.05	0.005
40 000	4000	400	40	4	0.4	0.04	0.004
30 000	3000	300	30	3	0.3	0.03	0.003
20 000	2000	200	20	2	0.2	0.02	0.002
10 000	1000	100	10	1	0.1	0.01	0.001

Multiplication square

×	1	2	3	4	5	6	7	8	9	10	11	12	13	14	15	16	17	18	19	20
1	1	2	3	4	5	6	7	8	9	10	11	12	13	14	15	16	17	18	19	20
2	2	4	6	8	10	12	14	16	18	20	22	24	26	28	30	32	34	36	38	40
3	3	6	9	12	15	18	21	24	27	30	33	36	39	42	45	48	51	54	57	60
4	4	8	12	16	20	24	28	32	36	40	44	48	52	56	60	64	68	72	76	80
5	5	10	15	20	25	30	35	40	45	50	55	60	65	70	75	80	85	90	95	100
6	6	12	18	24	30	36	42	48	54	60	66	72	78	84	90	96	102	108	114	120
7	7	14	21	28	35	42	49	56	63	70	77	84	91	98	105	112	119	126	133	140
8	8	16	24	32	40	48	56	64	72	80	88	96	104	112	120	128	136	144	152	160
9	9	18	27	36	45	54	63	72	81	90	99	108	117	126	135	144	153	162	171	180
10	10	20	30	40	50	60	70	80	90	100	110	120	130	140	150	160	170	180	190	200
11	11	22	33	44	55	66	77	88	99	110	121	132	143	154	165	176	187	198	209	220
12	12	24	36	48	60	72	84	96	108	120	132	144	156	168	180	192	204	216	228	240
13	13	26	39	52	65	78	91	104	117	130	143	156	169	182	195	208	221	234	247	260
14	14	28	42	56	70	84	98	112	126	140	154	168	182	196	210	224	238	252	266	280
15	15	30	45	60	75	90	105	120	135	150	165	180	195	210	225	240	255	270	285	300
16	16	32	48	64	80	96	112	128	144	160	176	192	208	224	240	256	272	288	304	320
17	17	34	51	68	85	102	119	136	153	170	187	204	221	238	255	272	289	306	323	340
18	18	36	54	72	90	108	126	144	162	180	198	216	234	252	270	288	306	324	342	360
19	19	38	57	76	95	114	133	152	171	190	209	228	247	266	285	304	323	342	361	380
20	20	40	60	80	100	120	140	160	180	200	220	240	260	280	300	320	340	360	380	400

This grid shows the connections between non-verbal reasoning skills.

If your child is having difficulties with a certain type of question, the links here can help you to guide them towards other areas to practise.

Page		Making connections	Common connections	Connections of direction, angle and symmetry	Finding similarities and differences	Spotting distractions	Breaking codes	Codes with two letters	Codes with three letters	Finding relationships	Changing shapes	Number and proportion	Moving and connecting shapes	Reflecting shapes	Rotating shapes	Spotting patterns	2 × 2 grids	3 × 3 grids	Completing sequences	Repeating patterns	One-step patterns	Two-step patterns	Number patterns
		40	40	40	41	41	42	42	43	44	44	44	44	45	45	46	46	47	48	48	48	49	49
40	**Making connections**																						
40	Common connections		●	◆	◆	◆		◆	◆		◆	◆	◆	◆	◆		◆	◆		◆	◆	◆	◆
40	Connections of direction, angle and symmetry		◆	●	◆	◆		◆	◆		◆		◆		◆		◆	◆					
41	Finding similarities and differences		◆	◆	●	◆		◆	◆		◆	◆	◆	◆	◆		◆	◆		◆	◆	◆	◆
41	Spotting distractions		◆	◆	◆	●		◆	◆								◆	◆					
42	**Breaking codes**																						
42	Codes with two letters		◆	◆	◆	◆		●			◆	◆	◆	◆	◆								
43	Codes with three letters		◆	◆	◆	◆			●		◆	◆	◆	◆	◆								
44	**Finding relationships**																						
44	Changing shapes		◆	◆	◆			◆	◆		●	◆	◆	◆	◆		◆	◆		◆	◆	◆	◆
44	Number and proportion		◆		◆			◆	◆			●								◆	◆	◆	◆
44	Moving and connecting shapes		◆	◆	◆			◆	◆		◆		●	◆	◆		◆	◆					
45	Reflecting shapes		◆	◆	◆			◆	◆		◆		◆	●			◆	◆				◆	
45	Rotating shapes		◆	◆	◆			◆	◆		◆		◆		●		◆	◆		◆	◆		
46	**Spotting patterns**																						
46	2 × 2 grids		◆	◆	◆	◆					◆		◆	◆	◆		●						
47	3 × 3 grids		◆	◆	◆	◆					◆		◆	◆	◆			●					
48	**Completing sequences**																						
48	Repeating patterns		◆		◆						◆	◆	◆		◆					●	◆	◆	◆
48	One-step patterns		◆		◆						◆	◆		◆	◆					◆	●		
49	Two-step patterns		◆		◆						◆	◆			◆					◆		●	
49	Number patterns		◆		◆						◆	◆								◆			●

◆ connecting skills   ● matching content pages

Now that your child has completed their practice they are ready to work with some example test papers.

These tests are created by publishers to give your child opportunities to experience what it is like to sit an actual 11+ test.

Choosing additional practice papers

Many schools use standardised 11+ tests and Letts produce a range of practice papers designed to provide your child with tests of the length and difficulty they are likely to encounter. These papers include…

- 11+ Practice Papers Standard Verbal Reasoning   9781844192410
- 11+ Practice Papers Standard Non-Verbal Reasoning   9781844192427
- 11+ Practice Papers Standard Maths   9781844192434
- 11+ Practice Papers Multiple Choice Verbal Reasoning   9781844192489
- 11+ Practice Papers Multiple Choice Non-Verbal Reasoning   9781844192496
- 11+ Practice Papers Multiple Choice Maths   9781844192502
- 11+ Practice Papers Multiple Choice English   9781844192519

Find out whether the school your child is applying to uses the standard papers *or* the multiple-choice papers and choose the relevant format; do not buy both, as they feature the same content.

If the school does not use these tests (they should give you this information), it is worth finding out whether you can obtain their past papers to review the content, difficulty and how they are laid out.

Reviewing the practice papers

As these papers come in sets of four, we suggest working with some of the papers in the following ways and saving one or two for 'real time' practice.

Without answering any of the questions, review the papers by looking at the areas outlined on this page. This exercise is to help your child understand how the papers are organised and the types of approaches that will work best with the different areas within each subject. This will also help them to manage their time more effectively.

Question focus

It is important to understand which skills the questions are targeting, so the first task is to identify the focus of each question.

Review each paper in the following way…

1 Look at the question to identify the skill being tested.

2 Review this against the relevant subject grids you have used for your child's Practice tests from the pull-out section (see pages 16–21).

3 List the skill against each question.

4 Review any questions that your child finds difficult to understand as you look through the paper. Refer to the relevant pages in Chapter *3 Reviewing your child's skills* pages for more details.

5 Follow up with further revision if necessary.

Identifying question types

In the 11+ papers your child will encounter questions in a range of styles. Examples of most of the different question types are included in the Practice tests in this book.

The second task is to identify the question types in the paper you are reviewing so that your child is aware of the possible variations.

Multiple-choice

Work out how the multiple-choice answer is indicated in each question.

1 List the instruction types you come across, such as 'circle', 'underline', 'write the answer in a box/on a line'.
2 Review different subject areas to see the range of instructions.

Standard

Not all papers will ask for standard (written) answers. However, when they do, the questions are often more challenging, so your child should be prepared for them.

1 Identify questions that require one word; a short phrase; longer answers requiring the identification of a range of points; and rewriting (or copying) a text to correct errors.
2 Review different subject areas to see the range of instructions.

Speed techniques

It is important for your child to be aware that the 11+ tests are timed and that speed and accuracy are considered in the selection process.

Reviewing the paper

Look through the test as a whole and work out how much time should be allowed to…

- review the whole paper quickly (we suggest two minutes on average)
- work through each page or section
- check through at the end (we suggest three minutes).

Note down some timings to refer to later on.

This exercise helps to build an understanding that spending too long on a tricky question can reduce the marks gained overall.

Order of questions

Being familiar with the layout of papers is very useful, as answering the easier questions first means gaining maximum marks. If your child runs out of time without tackling questions they are confident about, this will lead to fewer potential marks.

It may be worth identifying where in the tests there are multiple-choice questions – often your child will need less time to complete them.

Go through the tests with a highlighter and mark the easy questions to see if a pattern emerges.

Taking the practice papers

When your child is familiar with the format of the papers, they are ready to take a timed test in 'exam' conditions.

Using the information you have already gathered on the time they will need for certain sections, encourage your child to take the paper following these timings. Give them an analogue watch to check their progress.

They should spend the first two or three minutes…

- reviewing the complete paper
- looking for simpler questions to answer in each section first.

They should spend the last three minutes…

- checking the page numbering to make sure they haven't missed pages (it is easy to turn over two pages at once)
- checking that they have answered all the questions.

If there are questions that remain uncompleted in the given time, your child should tackle them later in order to gain practice in all the question types they are likely to encounter.

Reducing anxiety in the weeks before the tests is a difficult task for many parents. However, there are many activities you can do together that can help.

As your child should be confident in the skills they need to know by this point, you can build on their confidence by using puzzles, oral and verbal activities, and moving the focus away from written testing.

English

Researching collective nouns

Word games where the challenge is to invent new terms and words help to widen vocabulary and stimulate imagination for writing activities.

Finding collective nouns using the Internet leads to the invention of new ones. For example…

- What do you call a group of mobile phones? A chatter.
- What is the collective noun for computer games? A play.

Have fun thinking up new collective nouns for unusual groupings. For example, mobile phone masts, phone apps.

Colourful cars

Choose a car colour as you are driving along together. This game develops skills in considering a variety of adjectives and practice in alliteration.

Every time you see a car of that colour, take turns in adding another adjective beginning with the letter the colour starts with. For example…

Red car
Player 1: rusty red car
Player 2: revolting rusty red car
Player 1: revolving revolting rusty red car

Cartoon cut-outs

Find cartoon stories and ask your child to cut out the individual picture scenes and reorder them. This helps them to think up original ways to structure stories using flashback, time changes or dual action (where two events are happening in different places at the same time).

Maths

Multiple mania

Multiple mania is an excellent activity for practising counting in multiples.

Choose a vehicle with a set number of wheels. Count on by that number of wheels every time you see this type of vehicle. For example, if you choose a bicycle (two wheels), then every time you see a bicycle, add two to your total. This becomes more difficult when you choose a car!

Give me a sign!

To develop understanding of the properties of 2-D shapes, try looking for shapes as you drive along. This game is a challenging one.

Look for shapes with increasing numbers of sides on road signs. The shape should be named as it is spotted…

- one-sided shape (circle or ellipse)
- two-sided shape (a semi-circle)
- three-sided shape (a triangle).

You can also allow pub and restaurant signs. For example, a semi-circle could be a 'half moon'.

Top plates

There are many games you can play with car number plates and this one is useful for algebra practice. You will need a pencil and paper.

Write out the alphabet and assign a number to each letter, i.e. A = 1, B = 2. Each person chooses a number plate and converts the letters to numbers. The person with the highest score wins the round.

Alien attack!

Practise coordinate skills with this simplified version of 'Battleships'. The game is designed for two players.

Create four 6 × 6 grids – two for each player.

One grid is to record the 'hits' on your opponent, the other is to place your alien transport.

	1	2	3	4	5	6
F						
E						
D						
C						
B						
A						

Plot out your craft on your 'transport' grid, allowing the following number of squares for each. Make sure your opponent can't see this.

- Space buggy   1
- Flying saucer   2
- Space module   3
- Star ship   4

Take it in turns to call out a coordinate, e.g. B5; E4. If you make a hit you get another turn. The winner is the person who hits all their opponent's transport squares first.

Verbal reasoning

Words within words

You can play this game with any long words. Use the letters from the long word you have chosen to make new small words and see who can make the most new words. Letters can only be repeated in the small words if there is more than one within the long word.

Photosynthesis

the	pot	top
hot	hop	spot
tooth	photo	thesis
toy	toys	son
soy	nest	net

… you can probably find many more!

Word chains

Start a word chain using nouns. Each word has to start with the final letter of the previous word. For example…

Car   roof   fence   elephant   tiger racoon   nit   termite

Non-verbal reasoning

Any of these activities can help build skills in non-verbal reasoning…

- jigsaws
- memory game – a card game in which the object is to pair up cards bearing the same symbols by memorising where they are on the table
- spot the difference
- puzzle cubes.

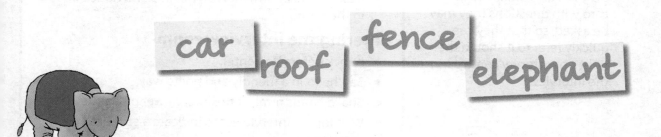

Many schools base their final selection on how well the applicants perform in an interview.

With the right preparation, your child can use this opportunity to show their potential to be a good member of the school and find out whether they will be happy there.

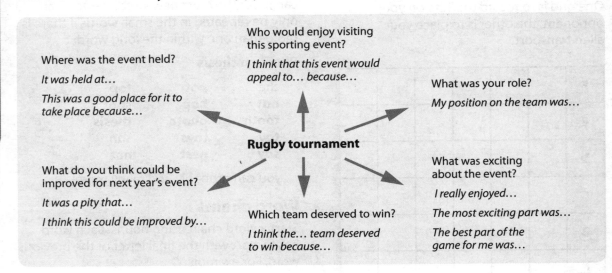

Where was the event held?

It was held at…

This was a good place for it to take place because…

Who would enjoy visiting this sporting event?

I think that this event would appeal to… because…

What was your role?

My position on the team was…

Rugby tournament

What do you think could be improved for next year's event?

It was a pity that…

I think this could be improved by…

Which team deserved to win?

I think the… team deserved to win because…

What was exciting about the event?

I really enjoyed…

The most exciting part was…

The best part of the game for me was…

Discussion topics

You can help your child prepare for the interview by making a web diagram of things that they could talk about.

If you have recently visited a sports match, museum, National Trust or English Heritage property, these make ideal topics to prepare for discussion.

Rather than asking them to make copious notes, help your child to complete a web diagram on a small index card with questions they may be asked, so that they can quickly refer to it should the right opportunity come up in the interview.

Meeting the interviewer

With your child, go through these tips on preparing to meet the interviewer.

Waiting

Calm yourself with these techniques when you are waiting to go into the interview room.

- Imagine you are holding an eggshell in each hand. This helps to relax your fingers and release tension.
- Breathe in slowly through your nose, counting to three, and then breathe out through your mouth at the same pace. Concentrate on your breathing to clear your mind.
- Do talk to other candidates who are waiting, but don't pester them for information.
- Read useful information on posters and notice boards in the room.

Entering the interview room

- Knock before you enter.
- Say 'hello' in a friendly and polite way.
- Shake hands firmly if the interviewer offers their hand.
- Wait for the interviewer to indicate a seat before you sit down.

First impressions
What to wear

First impressions are important. Find out in advance about the expected dress code. Your child's current school uniform is usually a suitable option.

- Make sure that the clothes they will be wearing are clean and ironed and that their shoes are cleaned and fastened securely.
- Make sure their hair is tidy and any fringe is trimmed in advance. If your child's hair is long, tie it back.

Creating an impression

Here are some tips to help your child create a good impression. Go through them together.

Body language

Interviews test your ability to communicate and body language can help you to do this if you appear relaxed, interested and confident.

Looking confident

- Sit in a relaxed way, but don't slouch.
- Sit so that your body, including your legs and feet, points towards the interviewer.
- Don't put up barriers by crossing your arms in front of you.
- Smile, but only when appropriate – don't just grin all the time.

Watch your hands

- Keep your hands away from your face and hair.
- Don't touch your nose before you answer a question.
- Use your hands to express yourself, keeping them folded at other times.

Keeping eye contact

- Look at the interviewer, but don't stare – remember to blink.
- Don't be tempted to look away if they ask a difficult question.
- Don't shut your eyes while you think about a question.

Communication skills

You are more likely to be able to both ask and answer questions if you are prepared. Researching information about the school in advance will help with questions on areas of interest to you such as sports and music. Your research will also make it easier to answer questions put to you.

Think about why you would like to go to the school, based on the information you have found out. It is important to be clear about your own views when talking about the school with the interviewer.

Avoiding yes/no answers

- Treat every question as an opportunity to tell the interviewer something about yourself.
- Try adding an example to your answer, or qualify it. For example, 'No, but…', 'Yes, although I sometimes…'

Answering and asking questions

- If you're asked about an area of weakness, explain how you've tried to improve.
- If you're asked a factual question and don't know the answer, say so.
- If you don't understand a question, ask for it to be repeated or ask for an explanation.
- Ask questions that show you have already found out something about the school and would like to hear more details than your research has provided.

Good interview technique is a skill and, like all other skills, can improve with practice.

Familiarity can reduce anxiety, and if your child has experience of how to deal with the interview experience they stand more chance of putting themselves across positively and confidently.

Preparing a mock interview

When your child feels confident in the preparations you have been through, consider preparing a mock interview so that they can experience the situation in advance. You could conduct this yourself or consider asking a good friend who your child knows well and feels confident with.

Setting

The aim is to make this a positive experience to build your child's confidence, but it should also simulate the situation they are likely to encounter, so the setting is important.

Choose a room that you are sure will be undisturbed for the 15–20 minutes you will need. Set the room out so there is somewhere for you to sit and go through your notes without your child seeing them and somewhere for your child to sit. There does not need to be a desk unless you feel more comfortable having somewhere to write.

Process

Copy out the interview checklist on page 69 to help you mark your child's performance. It is intentionally formal to help them become familiar with the structure of the interview process. That way, they can concentrate on what they have to say, rather than on what they have to do.

Make it clear to your child that you expect them to act as they would do in the real interview situation. For example, knocking before entering, greeting the interviewer and introducing themselves, as well as answering and responding positively to the questions.

Explain that you will be marking them on all aspects of the interview at the end and that you will go through the marks together so that you can talk about where they could improve.

Topics for discussion

Prepare a topic for discussion to form the main theme of the interview.

Choose a subject that you feel could be challenging but will enable your child to express their views. Do not simply choose a subject you know your child will have particular knowledge about as this will not be realistic practice for them.

The following opening sentences may give you some ideas.

'I am interested in hearing about what you would like to do with your life.'

'I'd like you to tell me about your personal heroes and heroines.'

'I'd like you to tell me about your current school.'

'People often joke about what they'd do if they ruled the world, but if you did, what would you do?'

'If you could choose, when and where would you prefer to live?'

Do not share the topic with your child before beginning the interview.

Range of questions

Consider and prepare a range of questions that fall into two categories:

A Questions that are open-ended and expect an explained response.

B Questions that could allow one-word answers but your child should be able to answer more fully without prompting.

Here are some examples of category A and B questions based on the discussion topic 'I'd like you to tell me about your personal heroes and heroines.'

Category A

- What do you think makes a hero or heroine? Give examples.
- What makes you say that?
- What do you think makes [your child's hero/heroine] a hero/heroine?
- If you had the power, how would you reward [your child's hero/heroine]?

Category B

- Do you think it's possible to be a hero or heroine in everyday life?
- Have you ever met a hero or heroine?
- Do you think you have ever behaved in a heroic way?
- Do you think heroes and heroines are always well-liked and happy?

Interview checklist

Prepare a checklist in line with this example that is relevant to your discussion topic.

Section A: Behaviour, demeanour and body language

Criterion	Mark available	Mark given
Knocks on door.	1	
Waits to be told to sit.	1	
Is calm, relaxed, does not fidget.	5	
'Open' body language – body pointing towards interviewer; not hunched with arms crossed in front.	5	
Is polite and friendly.	5	
Is enthusiastic.	5	
Remains calm under pressure.	5	
Total Section A		/27

Section B: Interview responses/content

Criterion	Mark available	Mark given
Gives a full response to both Category A and Category B, for example… Q: Do you think it's possible to be a hero or heroine in everyday life? A: Yes, look at firemen, for example.	5	
Gives reasons for opinions, for example… Q: What do you think makes [child's hero/heroine] heroic? A: Well, she stood up for what she believed in, and she didn't worry about what might happen to her.	5	
Listens to the questions and gives relevant and thoughtful replies, for example… Q: Do you think heroes and heroines are always well-liked and happy? A: Not always – Joan of Arc was burned at the stake, but she was a heroine to some people.	5	
Uses appropriate language (no slang, expletives, etc.) and expressive vocabulary (e.g. 'interesting'/'exciting', not 'nice'); understands any difficult words used by the interviewer.	5	
		/20

Once your child has taken the tests, the marking and admissions process begins.

Although you will need to wait to hear whether your child has been successful, you can spend some time becoming familiar with what happens next so that you will both be prepared.

Results for the 11+ tests do not come quickly! You should be prepared to wait between 10 and 16 weeks. If the school has not already informed you about when the results will be available, check the date with the school or the local education authority (LEA).

Understanding the results

The pass mark

The pass mark is determined by how many places are available at the school. Consequently, these often vary from year to year. If the school is co-educational, the pass mark for boys and girls may differ so that there will be a balanced year group.

Standardisation

In order to make the testing process fair, scores are standardised by age: this means that allowances are made for the younger children within the year group.

When the results are not as you expect

Offers from LEA schools

If you have applied to an LEA school, you will have selected up to three schools in order of preference.

If your child is not successful with their first choice, their name will be placed on the list for the next school you have specified. At this point, the second-choice school will take candidates who have put them as first preference so you are likely to be at the end of the list.

This will also apply to your third-choice school if your child is not successful with the second.

Offers from private and independent schools

If you have applied to a private or independent school you will not be offered an alternative school unless you have applied to them separately and your child has taken their 11+ tests as well.

Notification of appeals procedure

If your child was unsuccessful with an application to an LEA school, you should automatically receive details of the appeals procedure.

Although the appeals process is often described as informal, don't confuse 'friendly' with informal – this can be misleading. There is a formal timetable that must be adhered to and all paperwork will need to be submitted by the appropriate dates.

What to consider before appealing

Before making a formal appeal, you should consider the likelihood of success. If you have not been given the information, ask how close your child came to the pass mark.

Children who are close to the pass mark are sometimes offered a place on the waiting list. This is worth taking up as your child may still be successful – some of the accepted candidates may drop out.

Finding the admissions authority

The admissions authority is the body that sets the rules for school applications and admissions. Different types of schools have different authorities.

- For community schools and voluntary-controlled schools, this is the LEA.
- For voluntary-aided schools, foundation schools, trust schools, city technology colleges, academies and free schools, this is the governing body of the school in question.

Appealing the decision of LEA schools

The school will have decided on a number of criteria with which to assess appeals submitted. It is essential that you check the school prospectus to understand what these are before appealing. It is the job of the LEA to ensure that these criteria are applied impartially.

Parents are often asked to attend a meeting with the panel where they are allowed to ask questions and produce evidence to back the appeal. Any evidence you present will need to be sent to both the school and the panel before the meeting.

Specialist help

There are a number of specialist companies that can help you in putting your appeal together, or you can do this on your own. Organisations that can help with free advice include the Advisory Centre for Education (ACE). A wide selection of private companies specialise in supporting families in submitting appeals for a fee.

Putting the appeal together

Your appeal should clearly address all the criteria you have been asked to meet in the order in which they have been presented to you. This should be presented as a formal document. For example, if one of the criteria is that your home is within the catchment area, you should supply an Ordnance Survey map giving exact details of the distance from your house to the school to support your case.

Countdown to the hearing

- Once you have submitted your appeal, the admission authority must write to you at least ten school days before the hearing to confirm the date.
- At least seven school days before the hearing, the clerk must send you all the appeal documents to review. This will outline the school's reasons for being unable to offer your child a place.
- At least three school days before the hearing you will receive notification of who will be sitting on the appeals panel.

The appeal hearing

The appeal hearing can last from 30 minutes to two hours.

The panel for LEA schools is independent. After hearing your case, they will make their decision on the basis of whether your child or the school is likely to 'suffer' the most (for example, whether or not the addition of another child to the school would be problematic for the education of the existing intake).

Appealing the decision from other schools

Not all schools accept appeals, so you will need to contact the school in question to find out their procedure.

English

Comprehension 25

Finding information

1 **D:** Only James and Rob have actually held it: Mr Barry told Rob to put it in the desk; Ben and Pete tried to snatch it and didn't succeed.

Deduction and inference

2 Small pieces of paper (like confetti).

How writers use language

3 **D:** The answer is 'distracted'. 'Mislead' is not in the text.

Traditional and social context

4 The ten-shilling note James expected to see.

Grammar 26

Figurative language

1 **A:** Onomatopoeia is where a word mimics the sound.

Agreement in sentences

2 **B:** This is the only possible answer.

Punctuation 27

Basic punctuation

1 Mr Barry helped Rob to pick up the tin, its lid, the pieces of paper and the named glove lying next to them.

More about punctuation

2 **A:** The comma (B) should not be there. 'He' (C) should have a capital letter. 'Team' (D) shouldn't have a capital letter.

Spelling 28

Double letters and Tricky words (combined)

D: gnome, swimming

Question types 31

Comprehension

1 **C:** flashback

2 **B:** 1 and 5 only (explanatory texts, instructional and procedural texts)

Grammar

3 **E:** 'fiction' is a noun

Punctuation

4 **B:** There should be a comma before the speech mark.

Spelling

5 The aliens were hopping about on the roofs when a really cool ship flew by.

Maths

Numbers and their properties 32

Ordering and rounding whole numbers

1 -5, -4, -1, 0, 1, 2, 3, 7

Factors and multiples

2 **B:** Factors are numbers that multiply to give the number.

Calculations 33

Multiplying and dividing whole numbers

1 **C:** 13 755   this is half of 27 510, as 21 is half of 42

Algebra

2 **D:** $8n - 16 = 80$ $8n = 80 + 16$
$n = 96 \div 8$ $n = 12$

Fractions, decimals and percentages 34

Ratio and proportion

A: 18
$3 + 33 = 36$ litres altogether
To find out how many two-litre bowls can be filled, divide 36 litres by two.

Working with charts and data 35

Finding the mode, median, mean and range

1 **E:** The numbers should be arranged in order, including repeated numbers, so that the median can be found (the central value). As there are 14 numbers, the central value falls between two numbers, both of which are five, so the answer is five.
0 1 2 3 4 4 **5 5** 5 5 6 8 9 10

2 **A:** The range is found by subtracting the lowest value from the highest.
$10 - 0 = 10$

Probability

3 27 If two in every 18 receive a ticket, then Rajesh would get a ticket once in every nine visits. To get three tickets he will have to visit the shop 27 times (3×9).

Shape and space 37

Coordinates

(1, -2)   The line of symmetry goes through point (-2, 4), (-2, -2) so you count three squares to the right to find the answer.

Patterns and puzzles

2 3 One box is added horizontally for each number in the sequence. There is a red ellipse every other 'odd' square.

3 13 The formula to solve this is $N + 3$. The question asks about squares, not the shapes inside them.

Length, capacity and weight 38

Capacity

1 **D:** 2.75 litres = 2750 millilitres.
$2750 \div 50 = 55$

Time

2 00:00

Question types 39

Numbers and their properties

1 **D:** these are square numbers in reverse order
$11 \times 11 = 121, 10 \times 10 = 100$

Calculations

2 **A:** $7n - 4 = 52$ $7n = 52 + 4$
$n = 56 \div 7$ $n = 8$

Fractions, decimals and percentages

3 0.23, 32%, 46%, $\frac{23}{46}$, $\frac{2}{3}$, $\frac{9}{10}$

Working with charts and data

4 **D:** There are 13 fish in the tank, and five of these are red. This can be expressed as a fraction $\frac{5}{13}$

Shape and space

5 **B:** If the pool is rectangular, then the perimeter is ($2 \times$ width) + ($2 \times$ length). This can be represented by the sum…
$(15 + 15) + 2x = 90$
$2x = 90 - 30$ $x = 30$

Measuring

6 09.50; 09:50 or 0950 accepted.

Non-verbal reasoning

Making connections 41

Common connections

1 **b:** Shape b is the only shape without a line of symmetry. All the other shapes have at least one line symmetry.

Connections of direction, angle and symmetry/Spotting distractions

2 **a:** Shape a matches the two shapes on the left because it also has a right angle. The tints and rotations are both distractions.

Breaking codes 43

Codes with two letters

1 **c:** Q, R and P are the codes for the shape. X, Y and W are the codes for the shading pattern. The fifth shape is a triangle (R) and is shaded black (X). The answer is RX.

Codes with three letters

2 **a:** C, D and E are the codes for the shading pattern of the outer segments. A and B are the codes for the position of the shading patterns of the top segments. G, F and H are the codes for the shading pattern of the inner segments.
The fifth image's outer segments have a vertical striped pattern (E), its top left segment is not shaded, its top right segment is shaded (B) and its inner segments have a vertical striped pattern (F). The answer is EBF.

Finding relationships 45

Number and proportion

1 **b:** The images in the two example boxes both have nine vertices (corners). Answer b also has nine vertices.

Reflecting shapes

2 **c:** The images are reflected in a vertical mirror line and the colours are reversed. The rotated flags are distractions.

Spotting patterns 47

Simple 2×2 grids

1 **b:** Moving across the grid from left to right, the image in the box rotates 135° clockwise.

Simple 3 × 3 grids

2   e: The images in the boxes follow the rules… white in the first column, spotted in the second column, black in the third column. There is one shape in each box in the top row, two in the second row and three in the bottom row. As you go down the rows the images move one column to the left.

Completing sequences   49

Two-step patterns

1   c: The shapes in the boxes alternate between diamonds and pentagons. In pairs, the shapes alternate between black and white.

Number patterns

2   c: Moving across from left to right, the images in the boxes follow the sequence of a square being added to the bottom of the group on the left and another to the top of the group on the right. Each square that is added alternates with the previous one, black to white.

Question types   50

Making connections

1   d: Shape d has 11 corners like the two shapes on the left.

Breaking codes

2   e: H, I and J are the codes for the shading pattern. M, N and O are the codes for the type of triangle. The fifth shape contains a right angle (90°, N) and is shaded black (H).

Finding relationships

3   e: The shapes are brought together to form a regular shape, and the right-hand side becomes black.

Spotting patterns

4   c: The images in the boxes in the first column are reflected in a vertical mirror line into the last column.

Completing sequences

5   e: One circle is removed and one square is added each time. The colour does not change.

Verbal reasoning

Letter level   52

Making words across a gap

1   heel, thee   The elephant walked slowly through the grass. The elephant walked slowly through the grass.

Making two new words

2   cat thick   (**t**   chat   tick)

Analogies with letter changes

3   HJ   C is one letter ahead in the alphabet from B. E is one letter back in the alphabet from F. Applying the same rule to the example, then G is moved one letter ahead to give H. K is moved one letter back to give J.

Complete the third pair

4   star   The last letter is deleted and an 's' added to the beginning of the word.

Finding and reordering letters

5   LABORATORY   The scientist, and the fact he is going to a place combine to give a clue to the answer.

Word level   53, 54

Closest in meaning

1   cup, mug   Cup and mug are the only kitchen items that you can drink from.

Different in meaning

2   loud, quiet   Loud and quiet are the only words that are clearly opposite in meaning.

Analogies by word meaning

3   night, day   'Moon is to night as Sun is to day' are clear analogies.

Incomplete words

4   LIP   The boy SLIPPED on the wet mud. The position in the sentence of the word in capitals shows that it is a verb. The mud gives a clue to the answer.

Odd one out

5   jumper, trousers   All the other answers are types of fastening.

Compound words

6   understand
under + stand = understand

Word pairings

7   y   st<u>y</u>, <u>y</u>et   sk<u>y</u>, <u>y</u>es

Double meanings

8   bear   Bear can mean a type of animal or to carry something.

Word creation

9   mist   Counting from 1–8 across the two words, the letter order is 1, 6, 3, 4.

m o s t	m i s t	l i c k
1 2 3 4	1 6 3 4	5 6 7 8

Letter and number patterns   55, 56

Letters with number codes

1   B: Write the sum out in numbers first: 2 × 6 – 8 = 4, then convert back to a letter (4 = B).

Words with number codes

2   BAND
A = 1, B = 5, D = 6, N = 4, O = 3, S = 2

Alphabet pair sequences

3   DW: GT   First letter: counts forwards in the alphabet from A, B, C, D. The second letter counts backwards in the alphabet from Z, Y, X.

Letter codes

4   PRIM   The code letters GNRS are one letter backwards in the alphabet from the letters in the original word, HOST. To decode the letters OQHL move one letter forward in the alphabet to find PRIM.

Number sequences

5   64   Each number in the sequence is multiplied by two to give the next number.

Number patterns and equations

6   13   The last number in the outer brackets is subtracted from the first to give the answer in the middle brackets.
21 – 8 = 13

7   24   Left-hand side: (3 × 3) + 5 = 14
Right-hand side:
14 = (__ ÷ 2) + 2
14 – 2 = __ ÷ 2
12 × 2 = __
The answer is 24.

3 × 3 grids

8   There are several solutions to this question, including:

S	I	R
A	R	E
W	E	D

Logic   56

True statement

1   D: From the information given, the children can be arranged, from tallest to shortest, as follows: Inez and Pedro (the same height), James, Peter.

Deduction

2   52 minutes   If it took 10 minutes to walk to the shop, she arrived there at 3.40pm. She left 13 minutes later at 3.53pm. If she arrived home at 4.45pm, the time between leaving and arriving is 52 minutes.

Question types   57

Letter level

1   SUITCASE   The word 'packed' gives a clue to the answer.

2   trainer

Word level

3   thoroughfare   thorough + fare = thoroughfare

Letter and number patterns

4   LOAD   3254

5   1256
A = 5, D = 4, K = 6, L = 3, O = 2, S = 1

Logic

6   C: Matthew is always in bed by 8.50pm, Chrissy is in bed after 9.15pm on Thursday. These are the only facts we have been given so C, *Matthew is never late for bed on a school night*, is the only statement that fits this information. We don't know if Charlotte sometimes goes to bed late – we are told at the beginning that all the children should be in bed by 9pm on a school night but then told of an exception.

1 An answer that suggests that James was looking for money and there wasn't any, so he was angry and disappointed.

2 **D:** because the box was quiet when shaken

3 **E:** numerals

4 **C:** writing

5 **E:** 1 and 4 (The other boys are Rob, Pete and Ben.)

6 An answer that shows that James was angry or disappointed.

7 **C:** rapidly

8 He would have to have a pair of his own football boots.

9 An answer that shows that in the first paragraph the box is opened and in the second the box is shaken.
Both actions must be included to gain the mark.

10 **E:** adventure
The sub-title 'How it all began' suggests that this could be an adventure text and, of the list of options, this is the only one that could be correct. The strange numerals in the 'special' box suggest that there may be an adventure to come.

11 An answer that picks out the sub-title 'How it all began'.

12 **C:** going to look for something that isn't there

13 Suitable alternatives include: angrily, fiercely, viciously, wildly (or others).

14 **E:** The writer thinks the boy is a thief.

15 No, the writer doesn't like him. Mr Barry shouted ferociously, forced Rob into the playground and waved his cane at him.

16 The information that the adult had a cane would suggest that the story was set in the past.

17 **D:** Britain
The country the text is set in can be deduced from the names of the children and teacher, the language used and also the reference to 'Old Trafford'.

18 **D:** adverb

19 **B:** verb

20 **B:** waving a warning at him

21 **A:** the football boots that had shouted 'BUY US'

22 **C:** His

23 **A:** Wishing

24 **D:** had

25 **C:** I'll

26 **B:** are

27 **B:** were

28 **C:** about trigonometry, algebra

29 Mr Barnes helped Rob to pick up the tin, the lid, the pieces of paper and the named glove lying next to them.

30 Why had someone been so mean? Rob, the youngest in the class, could not hold back the tears.

31 It was quiet before Rob started to scream: Why? Why? Why?

32 **D:** items: a
My schoolbag always contains the same items: a pencil case, my football kit, a packed lunch and fruit juice.

33 **A:** James' box

34 The boys were playing with the **batteries** and the **torches** under the **arches** in the school chapel.

35 The **beginning** of the **lesson** was a disaster as Rob **rummaged** for the pieces of **paper**.

36 **E:** asassin; transfering. Correct spellings are **assassin; transferring**

37 **E:** He quick**ly** dis**a**greed with the **un**suitable secretary, while giving the small**est** of smiles.

38 He was hopeful that the energy-sav**ing** light bulbs would finally stop the care**less** waste of electricity.

39 The **museum's maintenance schedule** was very comprehensive, containing a list of **extraordinary** jobs, including cleaning the mummy.

40 **E:** Please don't postpone the meeting at the restaurant.

1 480 If the digit is less than 5, round down. If it is 5 or more, round up. 475 rounds up to 480.

2 3009 3099 3109 All the numbers have four digits and begin with the same number (3), so order the hundreds, tens and units values, not the thousands (3009, 3099, 3109, 3110, 3190, 3900).

3 30 The rule is +7.

4 The factors of 21 are 1, 3, 7 and 21.
$21 = 1 \times 21$ and 3×7

5 404
$200 + 100 = 300$
$50 + 30 = 80$
$7 + 8 + 9 = 24$
$300 + 80 + 24 = 404$

6 3 $5 \times 9 = 45$ and $48 - 45 = 3$

7 584
$70 \times 8 = 560$ ($7 \times 8 = 56$ and $56 \times 10 = 560$)
$3 \times 8 = 24$
$560 + 24 = 584$

8 56
$19 + 36$ (double 18) $+ 12$ (double 6) $= 67$
Use a number line and the rule 'Start at the Second number and Finish at the First number' (SSFF) to subtract 67 from 123.

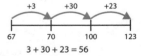

$3 + 30 + 23 = 56$

9 **B:** -3°C

10 $x = 5$ Subtract 7 from both sides to remove the 7:
$3x + (7 - 7) = 3x + 0 = 3x$
$22 - 7 = 15$
so $3x = 15$

Then divide both sides by 3 to find the value of x:
$3x \div 3 = x$
$15 \div 3 = 5$
so $x = 5$

11 $\frac{3}{5}$ A common multiple of the denominators 5 and 12 is 60 (5×12).
$\frac{7}{12} = \frac{35}{60}$ (multiply both numbers by 5)
$\frac{3}{5} = \frac{36}{60}$ (multiply both numbers by 12)
$\frac{36}{60}$ is larger than $\frac{35}{60}$ so $\frac{3}{5}$ is larger than $\frac{7}{12}$.

12 4 photographs
$\frac{1}{5}$ of 20 = 4, so $\frac{4}{5}$ of 20 = 16 (4×4)
$20 - 16 = 4$ photographs

13 12.87 Use a number line and the rule 'Start at the Second number and Finish at the First number' (SSFF).

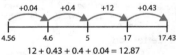

$12 + 0.43 + 0.4 + 0.04 = 12.87$

14 $\frac{4}{5}$ $0.8 = \frac{8}{10} = \frac{4}{5}$

15 130 10% of 650 = 650 ÷ 10 = 65, so 20% = $2 \times 65 = 130$

16 15 boys 5 groups of girls = 25
Each group = 25 ÷ 5 = 5
So 3 groups of 5 boys = 15

17 7 The first bar of the graph shows the result for cricket.

18 49 $7 + 13 + 11 + 4 + 14 = 49$

19 **C:** 16 The value that occurs most frequently in the list of data is 16. This is the mode.

20 **C:** $\frac{1}{4}$ Two numbers out of 8 (3 and 6) are multiples of 3.
$\frac{2}{8} = \frac{1}{4}$

21 **B:** 8 A cube has 8 corners.

22 **E:** Rectangle

23 **B:** 180° Full turn = 360°;
Half turn = 360 ÷ 2 = 180°

24 26cm Missing dimensions are
$2 + 3 = 5$cm and $8 - 5 = 3$cm.
The perimeter = $5 + 2 + 3 + 3 + 8 + 5$
= 26cm

25 (3, 4) 3 across, followed by 4 up.

26 The shape shaded black and to the left of mirror line AB is the translation of the original shape. The shape shaded black and to the right of mirror line AB is the reflection of the translated shape.

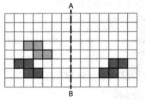

27

The columns are extended by 1 dot each time, and a column of dots is added. There are 2 dots in a column in the first pattern, and 1 column ($2 \times 1 = 2$ dots).
So in the second pattern there will be 3 dots in a column ($2 + 1$) and 2 columns ($1 + 1$), so $3 \times 2 = 6$ dots.

28 350cm There are 100cm in a metre so 3.5m is $3.5 \times 100 = 350$cm.

29 **C:** Medicine spoon
A bucket holds about 5000ml; a mug holds about 250ml; a saucepan holds about 3000ml; a soup bowl holds about 500ml.

30 1.05pm
08.50 + 4 hours
12.50 + 15 minutes 13.05 = 1.05pm

1 **b:** Image b is the only image where the two black (or white) rectangles are diagonally opposite. In all the other images the two black (or white) rectangles are next to each other.

2 **c:** Image c, if rotated (moved round), could not be mapped on to any of the other images. It has been flipped. All the other images would fit exactly on top of each other if rotated to the same position.

3 **d:** Image d has more than a half shaded black. The other images have exactly one half shaded. All the images have different sections shaded – this is a distraction.

4 **d:** Image d has a diamond-shaped arrow head. The other images have triangular arrow heads. The arrows are all pointing in different directions – this is a distraction.

5 **d:** Image d is an isosceles triangle and taller than all the other triangles. The other triangles are identical in size and shape – they are equilateral triangles. The arrangement of the triangles and shading patterns are distractions.

6 **d:** S, U and T are the codes for the shading patterns. V, W and X are the codes for the direction of the strip. The fifth shape has a diagonal strip going from top left to bottom right (X) and the strip has a striped pattern (T). The answer is TX.

7 **e:** O, M and N are the codes for the shape. Q, R and P are the codes for the shading pattern. The fifth shape is a rectangle (N) and is shaded black (R). The answer is NR.

8 **a:** A and B are the codes for the size of the image of the house. E, F and G are the codes for the number of windows. The arrangement of the doors and windows is a distraction. The fifth image is a large house (A) with two windows (F). The answer is AF.

9 **d:** B, C and A are the codes for the shading pattern of the bottom triangle. X, W and Y are the codes for the shading pattern of the top triangle. The fifth shape has a white bottom triangle (B) and a white top triangle (Y). The answer is BY.

10 **a:** E, F and G are the codes for the combination of shapes (outer and inner) within the boxes. L, B and K are the codes for the shading pattern of the inner shapes. S, U and T are the codes for the shading pattern of the outer shapes. The fifth shape is made up of trapeziums and squares (G). The inner shapes are spotted and white (B) and the outer shapes are black and striped (T). The answer is GBT.

11 **c:** Z, X and Y are the codes for the shape (above the face image). H, I and J are the codes for the direction of the mouth. C, D, E and F are the codes for the shading pattern of the shape. The fifth image has a rectangle above the face (X), the face has an upturned mouth (H) and the rectangle has a diagonal striped pattern (E). The answer is XHE.

12 **d:** The shape gets smaller and becomes white.

13 **c:** The number of shapes in the first box is squared (2 circles = 2^2 (2×2) = 4 circles; 3 triangles = 3^2 (3×3) = 9 triangles).

14 **d:** The shapes join together then rotate 180°.

15 **d:** The pattern within the boxes is reflected in a vertical mirror line. The direction of the shading pattern is also reflected.

16 **a:** The images within the boxes are reflected in a horizontal mirror line. Black shapes become white and white shapes become black.

17 **d:** The shape is rotated 90° anticlockwise.

18 **e:** The image in the box on the right is folded up to make the image in the box on the left.

19 **e:** The top shape in each box is reflected in a vertical mirror line while the bottom shape in each box is reflected in a horizontal mirror line (or rotated 180°).

20 **e:** As the images in the boxes move down a row they move one box to the right.

21 **e:** As the shield images in the boxes move down to the next row they rotate 45° anticlockwise but stay in the same column. As the smaller shapes move down to the next row they move one box to the left and rotate 45° anticlockwise.

22 **b:** The shaded outer segment within each box moves around the image, one segment at a time, in an anticlockwise direction. The shaded inner segment moves around the image, one segment at a time, in a clockwise direction. Black segments become spotted and spotted segments become black with each step.

23 **c:** The number of circles in the boxes increases by one each time; the circles are always positioned in the top left corner. White circles become black, black circles become white with each step.

24 **d:** A circle is added inside the smallest circle in the box, with all the circles touching at the bottom.

25 **b:** The image in each box rotates 45° clockwise each time.

26 **b:** The image in each box rotates 90° clockwise each time. The small black shape moves round three corners each time, in a clockwise direction.

27 **c:** A line moves from the top to the bottom of the box with each step, and the zig-zag line increases by two lines each time.

Verbal reasoning test answers

1   this   Both islands are beautiful.

2   ink seal   (**I**   link   sea)

3   **WT**   The first letter in each pair moves five places backwards each time. The second letter in each pair follows the same pattern so that the letters within each pair remain three letters apart.

4   firm   The final 'e' is removed from each word and replaced with 'm'.

5   HEDGEHOGS   The reference to prickles and hibernating are clues to the answer.

6   wide, broad   'Wide' means having a great distance from side to side, which has a similar meaning to 'broad'.

7   borrow, lend,   'Borrow' means to receive something on the understanding that you will give it back. This is opposite in meaning to 'lend' which means to give something to someone on the understanding that they will give it back to you.

8   lawn, tree   We mow the lawn to cut it and we prune a tree to cut it.

9   TEA   The concept of an old chair gives a clue to the word UNSTEADY.

10   cap, hat   These are items of clothing worn on the head. The others are worn elsewhere on the body.

11   notebook   note + book = notebook

12   **b**   rub, bib   sob, bar

13   fair   The word 'fair' has more than one meaning. It can mean that something is 'honest' or 'just'. It can also describe a community celebration like a 'carnival' or 'fete'.

14   glee   Counting from 1–8 across the two words, the letter order is 1, 3, 7, 5.

g a l e	g l e e	e v e n
1 2 3 4	1 3 7 5	5 6 7 8

15   **E:**   Write the sum out in numbers first: $3 \times 4 + 1 - 4 = 9$, then convert back to a letter (9 = E).

16   STOP
   O = 1, S = 3, P = 5, E = 6, T = 8

17   **FN**   The first letter in each pair moves ahead one letter. The second letter in each pair moves ahead two letters.

18   BYJLN   The code replaces each letter in the word with the letter that is nine ahead in the alphabet.

19   29   The pattern involves adding the first and second numbers to find the third, the second and third numbers to find the fourth, and so on.
   $1 + 3 = 4; 3 + 4 = 7; 4 + 7 = 11, 7 + 11 = 18, 11 + 18 = 29$

20   42   The number in the centre brackets is found by multiplying the outer numbers together. $6 \times 7 = 42$

21   11   Left-hand side: $(3 + 8) - 2 = 9$
   Right-hand side: $9 = (4 \times 5) - \underline{}$
   $9 = 20 - \underline{}$
   $9 + \underline{} = 20$
   The answer is 11.

22   Solutions to this question include:

B	U	N
O	R	E
A	N	T

23   **C:** *The friends ordered two pizzas between them.* Mark orders one pepperoni pizza and Joe and Jess order one vegetarian pizza; they order two pizzas in total, so this statement is true.

   Incorrect answers:

   A   *Mark, Joe and Jess all like pizza more than any other food.* Although the friends have chosen to go out for pizza, the text does not tell us that pizza is their favourite food.

   B   *Joe chose ham and pineapple pizza.* The text tells us that Joe shared a vegetarian pizza with Jess; it does not say he ordered ham and pineapple pizza.

   D   *Joe is vegetarian.* Just because Joe shared a vegetarian pizza does not necessarily mean he is vegetarian; he may simply prefer vegetarian pizza, or Jess might be vegetarian.

24   Wednesday
   Anna is busy on Mondays and Saturdays.
   Gina is busy on Tuesdays and Thursdays.
   Billy is busy on Thursdays and Fridays.
   Ash is busy on Fridays and Sundays.
   The only day that all of the friends are not busy is Wednesday.

Mental maths test answers

1   80   Rounding to ten. Numbers ending in 5 round to the ten above.

2   20 019

3   The factors of 18 are 1, 2, 3, 6, 9 and 18
   $18 = 1 \times 18, 2 \times 9$ and 3×6

4   131 $74 + 16 + 41 = 131$

5   88 $110 - 22 = 88$

6   126 $3 \times 40 = 120; 3 \times 2 = 6; 120 + 6 = 126$

7   70 $490 \div 7 = 70$

8   22 $(6 + 5) \times (4 \div 2) = 22$

9   $x = 12$ $4x = 48; 48 \div 4 = 12$

10   £7 $42 \div 6 = 7$

11   $1\frac{1}{4}$ $\frac{5}{4} = 1\frac{1}{4}$

12   9.9 $2.2 + 3.3 + 4.4 = 9.9$

13   40% $\frac{2}{5} = \frac{4}{10} = \frac{40}{100} = 40\%$

14   66% $100 - 34 = 66$

15   8   The ratio of green fish to red fish is 3 : 2
   Begin by finding out how many times three goes into 12.
   $12 \div 3 = 4$
   As there are four groups of three green fish there must be four groups of two red fish.
   $4 \times 2 = 8$

16   18   The range is calculated by subtracting the highest from the lowest number. **3** 4 7 8 19 **21**
   $21 - 3 = 18$

17   $\frac{5}{11}$ Divide the number of blue marbles by the total number of marbles to find the probability.

18   7

19   180°

20   18cm $3 \times 6 = 18$

21   64cm^2 $8 \times 8 = 64$

22   8 $11.5 - 4.5 = 7; 7 \div 2 = 3.5; 4.5 + 3.5 = 8$

23   8.5kg $17 \div 2 = 8.5$

24   320mm $32 \times 10 = 320$

25   29